# High-Quality
# Software Engineering

## Lessons from the
## Six-Nines World

*David Drysdale*

High-Quality Software Engineering: Lessons from the Six-Nines
World

Copyright © 2007 by David Drysdale

# CONTENTS

# 1  INTRODUCTION

Software is notorious for its poor quality. Buggy code, inconvenient interfaces and missing features are almost expected by the users of most modern software.

Software development is also notorious for its unreliability. The industry abounds with tales of missed deadlines, death march projects and huge cost overruns.

This book is about how to avoid these failures. It's about the whole process of software engineering, not just the details of designing and writing code: how to build a team, how to plan a project, how to run a support organization.

There are plenty of other books out there on these subjects, and indeed many of the ideas in this one are similar to those propounded elsewhere.

However, this book is written from the background of a development sector where software quality *really* matters. Networking software and device level software often need to run on machines that are unattended for months or years at a time. The prototypical examples of these kind of devices are the big phone or network switches that sit quietly in a back room somewhere and *just work*. These devices often have very high reliability requirements: the "six-nines" of the subtitle.

"Six-nines" is the common way of referring to a system that must have 99.9999% availability. Pausing to do some sums, this means that the system can only be out of action for a total of 32 seconds in a year. Five-nines (99.999% availability) is another common reliability level; a five-nines system can only be down for around 5 minutes in a year.

When you stop to think about it, that's an incredibly high level of availability. The average light bulb probably doesn't reach five-nines reliability (depending on how long it takes you to get out a stepladder), and that's just a simple piece of wire. Most people are lucky if their car reaches two-nines

| Reliability Level | Uptime Percentage | Downtime per year |
|---|---|---|
| Two-nines | 99% | 3.5 days |
| Three-nines | 99.9% | 9 hours |
| Four-nines | 99.99% | 53 minutes |
| Five-nines | 99.999% | 5 minutes |
| Six-nines | 99.9999% | 31 seconds |

**Table 1.1: Allowed downtimes for different reliability levels**

reliability (three and a half days off the road per year). Telephone switching software is pretty complex stuff, and yet it manages to hit these quality levels (when did your regular old telephone last fail to work?).

Writing software that meets these kinds of reliability requirements is a tough challenge, and one that the software industry in general would be very hard pressed to meet.

This book is about meeting this challenge; it's about the techniques and trade-offs that are worthwhile when hitting these levels of software quality. This goes far beyond just getting the programmers to write better code; it involves planning, it involves testing, it involves teamwork and management—it involves the whole process of software development.

All of the steps involved in building higher quality software have a cost, whether it's in development time or in higher salaries to attract and keep more skilled developers. This extra cost is the stake in a bet: a bet that the software is going to be successful and maintainable in the long run, and that the extra cost will be amortized over a longer lifetime for the software.

Lots of these techniques and recommendations also apply outside of this particular development sector. Many of them are not as onerous or inefficient as you might think (particularly when all of the long term development and support costs are properly factored in), and many of them are the same pieces of advice that show up in lots of software engineering books (except that here we *really mean it*).

There are some things that *are* different about this development sector, though. The main thing is that software quality is taken seriously by everyone involved:

- The customers are willing to pay more for it, and are willing to put in the effort to ensure that their requirements and specification are clear, coherent and complete.
- The sales force emphasize it and can use it to win sales even against

substantially lower-priced competitors.

- Management are willing to pay for the added development costs and slower time-to-market.
- Management are willing to invest in long-term development of their staff so that they become skilled enough to achieve true software quality.
- The programmers can take the time to do things right.
- The support phase is taken seriously, rather than being left as chore for less-skilled staff to take on.

Taken together, this means that it's worthwhile to invest in the architecture and infrastructure for quality software development, and to put the advice from software engineering books into practice—all the time, every time.

It's also possible to do this in a much more predictable and repeatable way than with many areas of software development—largely because of the emphasis on accurate specifications (see section 2.1, "Waterfall versus Agile").

Of course, there are some aspects of software development that this book doesn't cover. The obvious example is user interfaces—the kind of software that runs for a year without crashing is also the kind of software that rarely has to deal with unpredictable humans (and unreliable UI libraries). However, there are plenty of other places to pick up tips on these topics that I skip[1].

# 1.1  Intended Audience

## 1.1.1  New Software Engineers

One of the aims of this book is to cover the things I wish that I'd known when I first started work as a professional software engineer working on networking software. It's the distillation of a lot of good advice that I received along the way, together with lessons learnt through bitter experience. It's the set of things that I've found myself explaining over the years to both junior software developers and to developers who were new to carrier-class networking software—so a large fraction of the intended audience is exactly those software developers.

There's a distinction here between the low-level details of programming,

---

1    For example, on UI design I'd recommend reading Joel Spolsky's "User Interface Design for Programmers".

and software engineering: the whole process of building and shipping software. The details of programming—algorithms, data structures, debugging hints, modelling systems, language gotchas—are often very specific to the particular project and programming environment (hence the huge range of the O'Reilly library). Bright young programmers fresh from college often have significant programming skills, and easily pick up many more specifics of the systems that they work on. Similarly, developers moving into this development sector obviously bring significant skill sets with them.

The wider process of software development is equally important, but it's much less common for fresh new developers to have any understanding of it. Planning, estimating, architecting, designing, tracking, testing, delivering, and supporting software are not typically covered in a computer science degree. In the long term, these things are as important as stellar coding skills for producing high quality software.

This book aims to help with this understanding, in a way that's mostly agnostic about the particular software technologies and development methodologies in use. Many of the same ideas show up in discussions of functional programming, object-oriented programming, agile development, extreme programming etc., and the important thing is to understand

- why they're good ideas
- when they're appropriate and when they're not appropriate (which involves understanding why they're good ideas)
- how to put them into practice.

It's not completely agnostic, though, because our general emphasis on high-quality software engineering means that some things are unlikely to be appropriate. An overall system is only as reliable as its least reliable part, and so there's no point in trying to write six-nines Visual Basic for Excel—the teetering pyramid of Excel, Windows and even PC hardware is unlikely to support the concept.

## 1.1.2 Software Team Leaders

Of course, if someone had given me all of this advice about quality software development, all at once, when I started as a software developer, I wouldn't have listened to it.

Instead, all of this advice trickled in over my first few years as a software engineer, reiterated by a succession of team leaders and reinforced by experience. In time I moved into the position of being the team leader myself—and it was now my turn to trickle these pieces of advice into the teams I worked with.

A recurring theme (see subsection 1.2.3, "Developing the Developers") of this book is that the quality of the software depends heavily on the calibre of the software team, and so improving this calibre this is an important part of the job of a team leader.

The software team leader has a lot of things to worry about as part of the software development process. The team members can mostly concentrate on the code itself (designing it, writing it, testing it, fixing it), but the team leader needs to deal with many other things too: adjusting the plan and the schedule so the release date gets hit, mollifying irate or unreasonable customers, persuading the internal systems folk to install a better spam filter, gently soothing the ego of a prima-donna programmer and so on.

Thus, the second intended audience for this book is software team leaders, particularly those who are either new to team leading or new to higher quality software projects. Hopefully, anyone in this situation will find that a lot of the lower-level advice in this book is just a codification of what they already know—but a codification that is a useful reference when working with their team (particularly the members of their team who are fresh from college). There are also a number of sections that are specific to the whole business of running a software project, which should be useful to these new team leaders.

At this point it's worth stopping to clarify exactly what I mean by a software team leader—different companies and environments use different job names, and divide the responsibilities for roles differently. Here, a team leader is someone who has many of the following responsibilities (but not necessarily all of them).

- Designer of the overall software system, dividing the problem into the relevant subcomponents.
- Assigner of tasks to programmers.
- Generator and tracker of technical issues and worries that might affect the success of the project.
- Main answerer of technical questions (the team "guru"), including knowing who best to redirect the question to when there's no immediate answer.
- Tracker of project status, including reporting on that status to higher levels of management.
- Trainer or mentor of less-experienced developers, including assessment of their skills, capabilities and progress.

## 1.2  Common Themes

A number of common themes recur throughout this book. These themes are aspects of software development that are very important for producing the kind of high-quality software that hits six-nines reliability. They're very useful ideas for other kinds of software too, but are rarely emphasized in the software engineering literature.

### 1.2.1  Maintainability

Maintainability is all about making software that is easy to modify later, and is an aspect of software development that is rarely considered. This is absolutely vital for top quality software, and is valuable elsewhere too—there are very few pieces of software that *don't* get modified after version 1.0 ships, and so planning for this later modification makes sense over the long term.

This book tries to bring out as many aspects of maintainability as possible. Tracking the numbers involved—development time spent improving maintainability, number of bugs reported, time taken to fix bugs, number of follow-on bugs induced by rushed bug fixes—can quickly show the tangible benefits of concentrating on this area.

Fortunately, the most significant factor in maintainability is good design—and few people would argue that software needs good design. If the design clearly and coherently divides up the responsibilities of the different parts of the project, the chances of a later modification to the code being straightforward are much higher. On the other hand, it's always hard to tease a version 2.0 out of a design where the components are tangled together with complicated interactions and interacting complications.

The other main theme for maintainability is *communication*. The code itself only encodes what the machine needs to know; the programmers need to know much more—what code owns what resources, what the balance of pros and cons was between different approaches, in what circumstances the code is expected or not expected to scale well.

All of this information needs to be communicated from the people who understand it in the first place—the original designers and coders—to the people who have to understand it later—the programmers who are developing, supporting, fixing and extending the code.

Some of this communication appears as documentation, in the form of specifications, design documents, scalability analyses, stored email discussions on design decisions etc. A lot of this communication forms a part of the source code, in the form of comments, identifier names and even directory and file structures.

## 1.2.2 Knowing Reasons Why

Building a large, complex software system involves a lot of people making a lot of decisions along the way. For each of those decisions, there can be a range of possibilities together with a range of factors for and against each possibility. To make good decisions, it's important to know as much as possible about these factors.

It's also important to realize that this balance of factors is time-dependent: the most significant or relevant factors for the next three months are often radically different from the important factors for the next three years. For high-quality software development, this is particularly common—the long-term quality of the codebase often forces painful or awkward decisions in the short and medium term.

Scott Meyers has written a series of books about C++, which are very highly regarded and which deservedly sell like hot cakes. A key factor in the success of these books is that he builds a collection of rules of thumb for C++ coding, but he makes sure that the reader understands the *reasons* for the rule. That way, they will be able to make an informed decision if they're in the rare scenario where other considerations overrule the reasons for a particular rule.

In such a scenario, the software developer can then come up with other ways to avoid the problems that led to the original rule. To take a concrete example, global variables are often discouraged because they:

a)   pollute the global namespace
b)   have no access control (and so can be modified by any code)
c)   implicitly couple together widely separated areas of the code
d)   aren't inherently thread safe.

Replacing a global variable with a straightforward Singleton design pattern[2] counteracts a) and b). Knowing the full list allows d) to be dealt with separately by adding locking and leaves c) as a remaining issue to watch out for.

---

2   See Gamma, Helm, Johnson & Vlissides "Design Patterns".

### 1.2.3 Developing the Developers

It's generally well known[3], but bears repeating: the productivity of different software developers varies vastly. The best developers can be better than the average developer by an order of magnitude, and infinitely better than the worst developer.

This makes it obvious that the single most important factor in producing good software is the calibre of the development team producing it.

A lot of this is innate talent, and this means that recruitment and retention is incredibly important. The other part is to ensure that the developers you've already got are fulfilling all of their potential.

Programmers are normally pretty bright people, and bright people like to learn. Giving them the opportunity to learn is good for everyone: the programmers are happier (and so more likely to stick around), the software becomes higher quality, and the programmers are more effective on future projects because they're more skilled.

It's important to inculcate good habits into new programmers; they should be encouraged to develop into being the highest quality engineers they can be, building the highest quality software they can. This book aims to help this process by distilling some of the key ideas involved in developing top quality software.

All of the skills needed to write great code are not enough; the most effective software engineers also develop skills outside the purely technical arena. Communicating with customers, writing coherent documentation, understanding the constraints of the overall project, accurately estimating and tracking tasks—all of these skills improve the chances that the software will be successful and of top quality.

## 1.3 Book Structure

The first part of this book covers the different phases of software development, in roughly the order that they normally occur:
*   Requirements: What to build.
*   Design: How to build it.
*   Code: Building it.
*   Test: Checking it got built right.
*   Support: Coping when the customers discover parts that (they think) weren't built right.

---

3   See http://www.joelonsoftware.com/articles/HighNotes.html for an example.

Depending on the size of the project and the particular software development methodology (e.g. waterfall vs. iterative), this cycle can range in size from hours or days to years, and the order of steps can sometimes vary (e.g. writing tests before the code) but the same principles apply regardless. As it happens, high quality software usually gets developed using the apparently old-fashioned waterfall approach—more on the reasons for this in the Requirements chapter.

Within this set of steps of a development cycle, I've also included a chapter specifically on code reviews (see chapter 5, "Code Review"). Although there are plenty of books and articles that help programmers improve their coding skills, and even though the idea of code reviews is often recommended, there is a dearth of information on why and how to go about a code review.

The second part of the book takes a step back to cover more about the whole process of running a high quality software development project. This covers the mechanics of planning and tracking a project (in particular, how to work towards more accurate estimation) to help ensure that the software development process is as high quality as the software itself.

# 2  REQUIREMENTS

What is it that the customer actually wants? What is the software supposed to do? This is what requirements are all about—figuring out what it is you're supposed to build.

It often comes as a surprise to new developers fresh out of college to discover that the whole business of requirements is one of the most common reasons for software projects to turn into disastrous failures.

So why should it be so hard? First up, there are plenty of situations where the software team really doesn't know what the customer wants. It might be some new software idea that's not been done before, so it's not clear what a potential customer will focus on. It might be that the customer contact who generates the requirements doesn't really understand the low-level details of what the software will be used for. It might just be that until the user starts using the code in anger, they don't realize how awkward some parts of the software are.

Even if the customer does know what they want, they can't necessarily communicate this to the software development team. For some reason, geeks and non-geeks seem to lack a common language when talking about software. This is where the distinction between the *requirements* and the *specification* comes in: the requirements describe what the customer wants to achieve, and the specification details how the software is supposed to help them achieve it—customers who are clear on the former can't necessarily convert it into the latter.

Bug-tracking systems normally include a separate category for ignored bug reports where the code is "working as specified"—WAS. Much of the time, this really means NWAS—"not working, as specified": the code conforms to the specification, but the code's behaviour is obviously wrong—the specification didn't reflect what a real user needs.

For fresh-faced new developers, this can all come as a bit of a shock.

Programming assignments on computer science courses all have extremely well-defined requirements; open-source projects (which are the other kind of software that they're likely to have been exposed to) normally have programmers who are also customers for the software, and so the requirements are implicitly clear.

This chapter is all about this requirements problem, starting with a discussion of why it is (or should be) less of an issue for true six-nines software systems.

# 2.1  Waterfall versus Agile

*Get your head out of your inbred development sector and*
**look around[1].**

Here's a little-known secret: most six-nines reliability software projects are developed using a waterfall methodology. For example the telephone system and the Internet are both fundamentally grounded on software developed using a waterfall methodology. This comes as a bit of surprise to many software engineers, particularly those who are convinced of the effectiveness of more modern software development methods (such as agile programming).

Before we explore why this is the case, let's step back for a moment and consider exactly what's meant by "waterfall" and "agile" methodologies.

The waterfall methodology for developing software involves a well-defined sequence of steps, all of which are planned in advance and executed in order. Gather requirements, specify the behaviour, design the software, generate the code, test it and then ship it (and then support it after it's been shipped).

An agile methodology tries to emphasize an adaptive rather than a predictive approach, with shorter (weeks not months or years), iterated development cycles that can respond to feedback on the previous iterations. This helps with the core problem of requirements discussed at the beginning of this chapter: when the customer sees an early iteration of the code, they can physically point to the things that aren't right, and the next iteration of the project can correct them.

The Extreme Programming (XP) variant of this methodology involves a more continuous approach to this problem of miscommunication of requirements: having the customer on-site with the development team

---

1  Comment by Dave W. Smith on `http://c2.com/cgi/wiki?IsWaterFallDis`
`credited`

(let's call this the *customer avatar*). In other words: if interaction between the developers and the customer is a Good Thing, let's take it to its Extreme.

So why do most high-quality software projects stick to the comparatively old-fashioned and somewhat derided waterfall approach?

The key factor that triggers this is that six-nines projects don't normally fall into the requirements trap. These kind of projects typically involve chunks of code that run in a back room—behind a curtain, as it were. The external interfaces to the code are binary interfaces to other pieces of code, not graphical interfaces to fallible human beings. The customers requesting the project are likely to include other software engineers. But most of all, the requirements document is likely to be a reference to a fixed, well-defined specification.

For example, the specification for a network router is likely to be a collection of IETF RFC[2] documents that describe the protocols that the router should implement; between them, these RFCs will specify the vast majority of the behaviour of the code. Similarly, a telephone switch implements a large collection of standard specifications for telephony protocols, and the fibre-optic world has its own collection of large standards documents. A customer requirement for, say, OSPF routing functionality translates into specification that consists of RFC2328, RFC1850 and RFC2370.

So, a well-defined, stable specification allows the rest of the waterfall approach to proceed smoothly, as long as the team implementing the software is capable of properly planning the project (see chapter 8, "Planning a Project"), designing the system (see chapter 3, "Design"), generating the code (see chapter 4, "Code") and testing it properly (see chapter 6, "Test").

# 2.2  Use Cases

Most people find it easier to deal with concrete scenarios than with the kinds of abstract descriptions that make their way into requirements documents. This means that it's important to build some *use cases* to clarify and confirm what's actually needed.

A use case is a description of what the software and its user does in a particular scenario. The most important use cases are the ones that correspond to the operations that will be most common in the finished software—for example, adding, accessing, modifying and deleting entries in data-driven

---

2   The Internet Engineering Task Force (IETF) produces documents known as "Requests For Comment" (RFC) that describe how the protocols that make up the Internet should work.

application (sometimes known as CRUD: create, read, update, delete), or setting up and tearing down connections in a networking stack.

It's also important to include use cases that describe the behaviour in important error paths. What happens to the credit card transaction if the user's Internet connection dies halfway through? What happens if the disk is full when the user wants to save the document they've worked on for the last four hours? Asking the customer these kinds of "What If?" questions can reveal a lot about their implicit assumptions for the behaviour of the code.

As an aside, it's worth noting that these sample scenarios become very useful when it comes time to test the software (see chapter 6, "Test"). The scenarios describe what the customer/user expects to happen; the testing can then confirm that this is indeed what does happen.

## 2.3  Implicit Requirements

The use cases described in the previous section are important, but for larger systems there are normally also a number of requirements that are harder to distil down into individual scenarios.

These requirements relate to the average behaviour of the system over a (large) number of different iterations of various scenarios:

- Speed: How fast does the software react? How does this change as more data is included?
- Size: How much disk space and memory is needed for the software and its data?
- Resilience: How well does the system cope with network delays, hardware problems, operating system errors?
- Reliability: How many bugs are expected to show up in the system as it gets used? How well should the system cope with bugs in itself?
- Support: How fast do the bugs need to get fixed? What downtime is required when fixes get rolled out?

For six-nines software, these kinds of factors are often explicitly included in the requirements—after all, the phrase "six-nines" is itself an resilience and reliability requirement. Even so, sometimes the customer has some implicit assumptions about them that don't make it as far as the spec (particularly for the later items on the list above). The implicit assumptions are driven by the type of software being built—an e-commerce web server farm will just be assumed to be more resilient than a web page applet.

Even when these factors are included into the requirements (typically as a Service Level Agreement or SLA), it can be difficult to put accurate or realistic numbers against each factor. This may itself induce another implicit requirement for the system—to build in a way of generating the quantitative data that is needed for tracking. An example might be to include code to measure and track response times, or to include code to make debugging problems easier and swifter (see subsection 3.2.4, "Diagnostics"). In general, SLA factors are much easier to deal with in situations where there is existing software and tracking systems to compare the new software with.

# 3  DESIGN

The process of making a software product is sometimes compared to the process of making a building. This comparison is sometimes made to illustrate how amateurish and unreliable software engineering is in comparison to civil engineering, with the aim of improving the former by learning lessons from the latter.

However, more alert commentators point out that the business of putting up buildings is only reliable and predictable when the buildings are the same as ones that have been done before. Look a little deeper, into building projects that are the first of their kind, and the industry's reputation for cost overruns and schedule misses starts to look comparable with that of the software industry.

A new piece of software is almost always doing something new, that hasn't been done in exactly that way before. After all, if it were exactly the same as an existing piece of software, we could just reuse that software—unlike buildings, it's easy to copy the contents of a hard drive full of code.

So designing large, complex systems from scratch is hard—whether in software engineering or civil engineering. For software, there is only one technique that can tame this difficulty: *divide and conquer*. The main problem gets broken down into a collection of smaller problems, together with their interactions. These smaller problems get subdivided in turn, and the process repeats until the individual sub-sub-problems are tractable on their own (and some of these may even be problems that have been solved before, whose solutions can be re-used).

Tractable for the humans building the system, that is. This process of subdivision is much more about making the system comprehensible for its designers and builders, than about making the compiler and the microprocessor able to deal with the code. The underlying hardware can cope with any amount of spaghetti code; it's just the programmers that can't cope with trying to build a stable, solid system out of spaghetti. Once a system reaches a certain critical mass, there's no way that the developers can hold all of the system in their heads at once without some of the spaghetti sliding out of their ears[1].

Software design is all about this process of dividing a problem into the appropriate smaller chunks, with well-defined, understandable interfaces between the chunks. Sometimes these chunks will be distinct executable files, running on distinct machines and communicating over a network. Sometimes these chunks will be *objects* that are distinct instances of different classes, communicating via method calls. In every case, the chunks are small enough that a developer can hold all of a chunk in their head at once—or can hold the *interface* to the chunk in their head so they don't need to understand the internals of it.

Outside of the six-nines world of servers running in a back room, it's often important to remember a chunk which significantly affects the design, but which the design has less ability to affect: the User. The design doesn't describe the internals of the user (that would biology, not engineering) but it does need to cover the interface to the user,

This chapter discusses the principles behind good software design— where "good" means a design that has the highest chance of working correctly, being low on bugs, being easy to extend in the future, and implemented in the expected timeframe. It also concentrates on the specific challenges that face the designers of highly resilient, scalable software.

Before moving on to the rest of the chapter, a quick note on terminology. Many specific methodologies for software development have precise meanings for terms like "object" and "component"; in keeping with the methodology-agnostic approach of this book, these terms (and others, like "chunk") are used imprecisely here. At the level of discussion in this chapter, if the specific difference between an object and a component matters, you're probably up to no good.

# 3.1  Interfaces and Implementations

The most important aspect of the division of a problem into individual components is the separation between the interface and the implementation of each component.

The interface to a component is built up of the operations that the com-

---

1   Apologies if that's an image you're now trying desperately trying to get out of your head.

ponent can perform, together with the information that other components (and their programmers) need to know in order to successfully use those operations. For the outermost layer of the software, the interface may well be the User Interface, where the same principle applies—the interface is built up of the operations that the user can perform with the keyboard and mouse—clicking buttons, moving sliders and typing command-line options.

As ever, the definition of the "interface" to a component or an object can vary considerably. Sometimes the interface is used to just mean the set of public methods of an object; sometimes it is more comprehensive and includes pre-conditions and post-conditions (as in Design By Contract) or performance guarantees (such as for the C++ STL); sometimes it includes aspects that are only relevant to the programmers, not the compiler (such as naming conventions[2]). Here, we use the term widely to include all of these variants—including more nebulous aspects, such as comments that hint on optimal use of the interface.

The implementation of a component is of course the chunk of software the fulfils the interface. This typically involves both code and data; as Niklaus Wirth has observed, "Algorithms + Data Structures = Programs".

The interface and the implementation should be as distinct as possible, as discussed later (see subsection 3.1.2, "Black Box Principle"). If they aren't distinct, then the component isn't really part of a subdivision of the overall problem into smaller chunks: none of the other chunks in the system can just use the component as a building block, because they have to understand something about how the building block is itself built.

## 3.1.1  Good Interface Design

So, what makes a good interface for a software component?

The interface to a software component is there to let other chunks of software use the component. As such, a good interface is one that makes this easier, and a bad interface is one that makes this harder. This is particularly important in the exceptional case that the interface is to the user rather than another piece of software.

The interface also provides an abstraction of what the internal implementation of the component does. Again, a good interface makes this internal implementation easier rather than harder; however, this goal is

---

2  For example, the Scheme programming language ends all predicates with a question mark (null?) and all functions that have side effects with an exclamation mark (vector-set!).

often at odds with the previous goal.

There are several principles that help to make an interface optimal for its clients—where the "client" of an interface includes both the other chunks of code that use the interface, and the programmers that write this code.

- *Clear Responsibility.* Each chunk of code should have a particular job to do, and this job should boil down to a single clear responsibility (see subsection 3.2.1, "Component Responsibility").

- *Completeness.* It should be possible to perform any operation that falls under the responsibility of this component. Even if no other component in the design is actually going to use this particular operation, it's still worth sketching out the interface for it. This provides reassurance that it will be possible to extend the implementation to that operation in the future, and also helps to confirm that the component's particular responsibilities are clear.

- *Principle of Least Astonishment.* The interface to a component needs to be written relative to the expectations of the clients—who should be assumed to know nothing about the internals of the component. This includes expectations about resource ownership (whose job is to release resources?), error handling (what exceptions are thrown?), and even cosmetic details such as conformance to standard naming conventions and terminology for the local environment.

To ensure that an interface makes the implementation as easy as possible, it needs to be *minimal.* The interface should provide all the operations that its clients might need (see *Completeness* above), but no more. The principle of having clear responsibilities (see above) can help to spot areas of an interface that are actually peripheral to the core responsibility of a component—and so should be hived off to a separate chunk of code.

For example, imagine a function that builds a collection of information describing a person (probably a function like `Person::Person` in C++ terms), including a date of birth. The chances are (sadly) that there are likely to be many different ways of specifying this date—should the function cope with all of them, in different variants, in order to be as helpful as possible for the clients of the function?

In this case, the answer is no. The core responsibility of the function is to build up data about people, not to do date conversion. A much better approach is to pick one date format for the interface, and separate out all of the date conversion code into a separate chunk of code. This separate chunk has one job to do—converting dates—and is very likely to be useful elsewhere in the overall system.

## 3.1.2  Black Box Principle

The client of a component shouldn't have to care how that component is implemented. In fact, it shouldn't even *know* how the component is implemented—that way, there's no temptation to rely on internal implementation details.

This is the black box principle. Clients of a component should treat it as if it were a black box with a bunch of buttons and controls on the outside; the only way to get it to do anything is by frobbing these externally visible knobs. The component itself needs to make enough dials and gauges visible so that its clients can use it effectively, but no more than that.

This principle gives us a good way of testing whether we have come up with a good interface or not: is it possible to come up with a completely different implementation that still satisfies the interface? If so, then there's a good chance that the component's interface will be robust to changes in future—after all, if the entire internal gubbins of the component could be replaced without anyone noticing, the chances are that any future enhancement will also have no detrimental effect.

## 3.1.3  Physical Architecture

The physical architecture of a software system covers all of the things that the code needs to interface with in order to go from source code to a running system—machines, power supplies, hard disks, networks, compilers, linkers, peripherals.

This is often an area that's taken for granted; for a desktop application, the physical architecture is just likely to involve decisions about which directories to install code into, how to divide the code up into different shared libraries, and which operating systems to support.

For six-nines software, however, these kinds of physical factors are typically much more important in the design of such systems:

- They often combine hardware and software together as a coherent system, which can involve much lower-level considerations about what code runs where, and when.
- They often have scalability requirements that necessitate running on multiple machines in parallel—which immediately induces problems with keeping data synchronized properly.
- They are often large-scale software systems where the sheer weight of code causes problems for the toolchains. A build cycle that takes

a week to run can seriously impact development productivity[3].

* The reliability requirements often mean that the code has to transparently cope with software and hardware failures, and even with modifications of the running software while it's running.

For these environments, each software component's interface to the non-software parts of the system becomes important enough to require detailed design consideration—and the interfaces between software components may have hardware issues to consider too.

To achieve true six-nines reliability, every component of the system has to reach that reliability level. This involves a lot of requirements on the whole hardware platform—the power supply, the air conditioning, the rack chassis, the processor microcode, the operating system, the network cards—which are beyond the scope of this book.

# 3.2   Designing for the Future

Successful software has a long lifetime; if version 1.0 works well and sells, then there will be a version 2.0 and a version 8.1 and so on. As such, it makes sense to plan for success by ensuring that the software is designed with future enhancements in mind.

This section covers the key principles involved in "designing in the future tense": putting in effort today so that in years to come all manner of enhancements Should Just Work.

## 3.2.1   Component Responsibility

The most important factor that eases future modifications to software is clear responsibilities for each of the components of the system (see subsection 3.1.1, "Good Interface Design"). What data does it hold; what processing does it perform; most importantly, what *concept* does it correspond to?

When a new aspect of functionality is needed, the designer can look at the responsibilities of the existing components. If the new function fits under a particular component's aegis, then that's where the new code will be implemented. If no component seems relevant, then a new component may well be needed.

For example, the Model-View-Controller architectural design pattern

---

3   John Lakos' "Large Scale C++ Software Design" is possibly the only book that addresses this issue in depth; if your system has this sort of problem (even if it's not a C++ system), it's well worth reading.

is a very well-known example of this (albeit from outside the world of six-nines development). Roughly:

- The Model is responsible for holding and manipulating data.
- The View is responsible for displaying data to the user.
- The Controller is responsible for converting user input to changes in the underlying data held by the Model, or to changes in how it is displayed by the View.

For any change to the functionality, this division of responsibilities usually makes it very clear where the change should go.

## 3.2.2 Minimizing Special Cases

> *"I laughed heartily as I got questions from one of my former employees about FTP code the he was rewriting. It had taken 3 years of tuning to get code that could read the 60 different types of FTP servers, those 5000 lines of code may have looked ugly, but at least they worked."* – Lou Montulli

A special case in code is an interruption to the clear and logical progression of the code. A prototypical toy example of this might be a function that returns the number of days in a month: what does it return for February? All of sudden, a straightforward array-lookup from month to length won't work; the code needs to take the year as an input and include an if (month == February) arm that deals with leap years.

An obvious way to spot special cases is by the presence of the words "except" or "unless" in a description of some code: this function does X except when Y.

Special cases are an important part of software development. Each special case in the code reflects something important that has been discovered during the software development process. This could be a particular workaround for a bug in another product, an odd wrinkle in the specification, or an ineluctable feature of the real world (like the leap year example above).

However, special cases are distressing for the design purist. Each special case muddies the responsibilities of components, makes the interface less clear, makes the code less efficient and increases the chances of bugs creeping in between the edge cases.

So, accepting that special cases are unavoidable and important, how can software be designed to minimize their impact?

An important observation is that special cases tend to accumulate as software passes through multiple versions. Version 1.0 might have only had three special cases for interoperating with old web server software, but by version 3.4 there are dozens of similar hacks.

This indicates the most effective mechanism for dealing with special cases: generalize them and encapsulate the generalized version in a single place. For the leap year example, this would be the difference between `if (month == February)` and `if (IsMonthOfVaryingLength(month))` (although this isn't the best example to use, since there are unlikely to be any changes in month lengths any time soon).

## 3.2.3 Scalability

Successful software has a long lifetime (see section 3.2, "Designing for the Future"), as new functionality is added and higher version numbers get shipped out of the door. However, successful software is also popular software, and often the reason for later releases is to cope with the consequences of that popularity.

This is particularly relevant for server-side applications—code that runs on backend web servers, clusters or even mainframes. The first version may be a single-threaded single process running on such a server. As the software becomes more popular, this approach isn't able to keep up with the demand.

So the next versions of the software may need to become multithreaded (but see section 4.3, "Multithreading"), or have multiple instances of the program running, to take advantage of a multiprocessor system. This requires *synchronization*, to ensure that shared data never gets corrupted. In one process or on one machine, this can use the synchronization mechanisms provided by the environment: semaphores and mutexes, file locks and shared memory.

As the system continues to be successful, even this isn't good enough—the system needs to be *distributed*, with the code running on many distinct machines, carefully sharing data between the machines in a synchronized way. This is harder to achieve, because there are far fewer synchronization primitives to rely on.

Let's suppose the software is more successful still, and customers are now relying on the system 24 hours a day, 7 days a week—so we're now firmly in the category of four-nines, five-nines or even six-nines software. What happens if a fuse blows in the middle of a transaction, and one of the machines comes down? The system needs to be *fault tolerant*, failing the transaction smoothly over to another machine.

Worse still, how do you upgrade the system in a 24/7 environment? The running code needs to be swapped for the new code, in a seamless way that also doesn't corrupt any data or interrupt any running transactions: a *dynamic software upgrade*. Of course, nothing is perfect—chances are that sometimes the dynamic software upgrade system will also need to cope with a dynamic software *downgrade* to roll the new version back to the drawing board.

A few of these evolutionary steps can apply to single-user desktop applications too. Once lots of versions of a product have been released, it's all too easy to have odd interactions between incompatible versions of code installed at the same time (so-called "DLL Hell"). Similarly, power users can stretch the performance of an application and wonder why their dual-CPU desktop isn't giving them any benefits[4].

Having a good design in the first case can make the whole scary scalability evolution described above go much more smoothly than it would otherwise do—and is essential for six-nines systems where these scalability requirements are needed even in the 1.0 version of the product.

Because this kind of scaling-up is so important in six-nines systems, a whole section later in this chapter (see section 3.3, "Scaling Up") is devoted to the kinds of techniques and design principles that help to achieve this. For the most part, these are simple slants to a design, which involve minimal adjustments in the early versions of a piece of software but which can reap huge rewards if and when the system begins to scale up massively.

As with software specifications (see section 2.1, "Waterfall versus Agile"), it's worth contrasting this approach with the current recommendations in other software development sectors. The Extreme Programming world has a common precept that contradicts this section: You Aren't Going to Need It (YAGNI). The recommendation here is *not* to spend much time ensuring that your code will cope with theoretical future enhancements: code as well as possible for today's problems, and sort out tomorrow's problems when they arrive—since they will probably be different from what you expected when they do arrive.

For six-nines systems, the difference between the two approaches is again driven by the firmness of the specification. Such projects are generally much more predictable overall, and this includes a much better chance of correctly predicting the ways that the software is likely to evolve. Moreover, for large and complex systems the kinds of change described in this section are extraordinarily difficult to retro-fit to software that has

---

4    In 2000, the member of staff with the most highly powered computer at the software development house I worked was the technical writer—Microsoft Word on a 1500 page document needs a lot of horsepower.

not been designed to allow for them—for example, physically dividing up software between different machines means that the interfaces have to change from being synchronous to asynchronous (see subsection 3.3.2, "Asynchronicity").

So, (as ever) it's a balance of factors: for high-resilience systems, the probability of correctly predicting the future enhancements is higher, and the cost of not planning for the enhancements is much higher, so it makes sense to plan ahead.

## 3.2.4  Diagnostics

Previous sections have described design influences arising from planning for success; it's also important to plan for failure.

All software systems have bugs. It's well known that it's much more expensive to fix bugs when they're out in the field, and so a lot of software engineering practices are aimed at catching bugs as early as possible in the development process. Nevertheless, it is inevitable that bugs will slip out, and it's important to have a plan in place for how to deal with them.

In addition to bugs in the software, there are any number of other factors that can stop software from working correctly out in the field. The user upgrades their underlying operating system to an incompatible version; the network cable gets pulled out; the hard disk fills up, and so on.

Dealing with these kinds of circumstances is much easier if some thought has been put into the issue as part of the design process. It's straightforward to build in a logging and tracing facility as part of the original software development; retrofitting it after the fact is much more difficult. This diagnostic functionality can be useful even before the software hits the field—the testing phase (see chapter 6, "Test") can also take advantage of it.

Depending on the environment that the software is expected to run in, there are a number of diagnostic areas to be considered as part of the design.

- Installation verification: checking that all the dependencies for the software are installed, and that all versions of the software itself match up correctly.
- Tracing and logging: providing a system whereby diagnostic information is produced, and can be tuned to generate varying amounts of information depending on what appears to be the problem area. This can be particularly useful for debugging crashed code, since core files/crash dumps are not always available.

- Manageability: providing a mechanism for administrators to reset the system, or to prune particularly problematic subsets of the software's data, aids swift recovery from problems as they happen.
- Data verification: internal checking code that confirms whether chunks of data remain internally consistent and appear to be uncorrupted.
- Batch data processing: providing a mechanism to reload large amounts of data can ease recovery after a disastrous failure (you did remember to include a way to back up the data from a running system, didn't you?).

## 3.2.5  Avoiding the Cutting Edge

Programmers are always excited by new toys. Sadly, this extends to software design too: developers often insist on the very latest and shiniest tools, technologies and methodologies.

However, the risks and costs associated with these cutting edges is seldom calculated correctly. New tools are more likely to be incomplete and bug-ridden; their support for varying operating systems and programming languages can be patchy (which leads to extensibility problems in future). For high quality software, the overall reliability is only as good as the weakest link in the whole system, and using the latest and greatest technology hugely increases the chance that the weakest link will be in code that you have no control over.

In the longer term, working with the very latest in technology is also a wager. Many technologies are tried; few survive past their infancy, which causes problems if your software system relies on something that has had support withdrawn.

It's not just the toolchain that may have problems supporting the latest technology: similar concerns apply to the developers themselves. Even if the original development team fully understand the new technology, the maintainers of version 1.0 and the developers of version 2.0 might not— and outside experts who can be hired in will be scarce (read: expensive).

Even if the technology in question is proven technology, if the team doing the implementation isn't familiar with it, then some of the risks of cutting edge tools/techniques apply. In this situation, this isn't so much a reason to avoid the tools, but instead to ensure that the project plan (see chapter 8, "Planning a Project") allows sufficient time and training for the team to get to grips with the technology.

So when is new technology appropriate? Obviously, prototypes and small-scale systems allow a lot more opportunity for experimentation with lower risk. The desire of the programming team to expand their skill set and learn something new and different is also a significant factor. Allowing experimentation means that the team will be happier (see section 9.4, "Personnel Development") and the next time round, the technology will no longer be untried: the cutting edge will have been blunted.

# 3.3  Scaling Up

An earlier section discussed the importance of planning ahead for scalability. This section describes the principles behind this kind of design for scalability—principles which are essential to achieve truly resilient software.

## 3.3.1  Good Design

The most obvious aspect of designing for scalability is to ensure that the core design is sound. Nothing highlights potential weak points in a design better that trying to extend it to a fault-tolerant, distributed system.

The first part of this is clarity of interfaces—since it is likely that these interfaces will span distinct machines, distinct processes or distinct threads as the system scales up.

Another key aspect that helps to ease the transition to distributed or resilient systems is to carefully encapsulate access to data, so a single set of components have clear responsibility for this. If every chunk of code that reads or writes persistent data does so through a particular well-defined interface (as for the Model part of a Model/View/Controller system), then it's much easier to convert the underlying data access component from being flat-file based to being database driven, then to being remote-distributed-database driven—without changing any of the other components.

Likewise, if all of the data that describes a particular transaction in progress is held together as a coherent chunk, and all access to it is through known, narrow interfaces, then it is easier to monitor that state from a different machine—which can then take over smoothly in the event of failure.

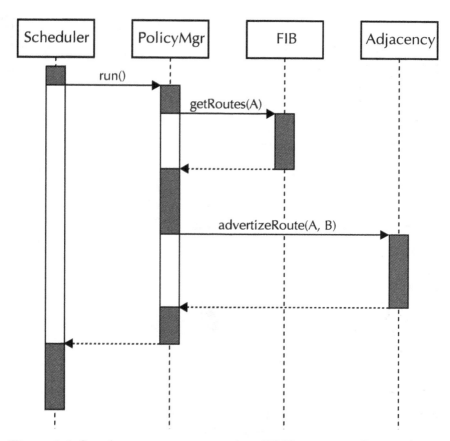

**Figure 3.1: Synchronous interaction (as a UML sequence diagram)**

## 3.3.2 Asynchronicity

A common factor in most of the scalability issues discussed in this chapter is the use of asynchronous interfaces rather than synchronous ones. Asynchronous interfaces are harder to deal with, and they have their own particular pitfalls that the design of the system needs to cope with.

A synchronous interface is one where the results of the interface come back immediately (or apparently immediately). An interface made up of function calls or object method calls is almost always synchronous—the user of the interface calls the function with a number of parameters, and when the function call returns the operation is done.

An asynchronous interface involves a gap between the invocation and the results. The information that the operation on the interface needs is

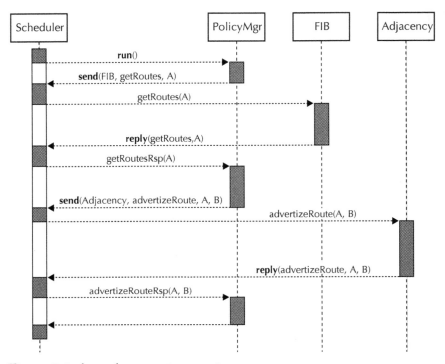

**Figure 3.2: Asynchronous interaction**

packaged up and delivered, and some time later the operation takes place and any results are delivered back to the code that uses the interface. This is usually done by encapsulating the interface with some kind of message-passing mechanism.

This immediately makes things much more complicated.

- There has to be some method for the delivery of the results. This could be the arrival of a message, or an invocation of a registered callback, but in either case the scheduling of this mechanism has to be set up.
- The results are delivered back to a different part of the code rather than just the next line, destroying locality of reference.
- The code that invokes the asynchronous operation needs to hold on to all of the state information associated with the operation while it's waiting for the results.
- When the results of an operation arrive, they have to be correlated with the information that triggered that operation. What happens if the same operation occurs multiple times in parallel with different

data?

- The code has to cope with a variety of timing windows, such as when the answers to different operations return in a different order, or when state needs to be cleaned up because the provider of the interface goes away while operations are pending.

Asynchronous interfaces are ubiquitous in highly resilient systems. If data is distributed among different processors and machines, then that data needs make its way to the appropriate machine—which is inherently asynchronous. Likewise a backup system, waiting in the wings to take over should the primary machine fail, can only be kept up to date via an asynchronous mechanism.

Asynchronicity turns up elsewhere too. Graphical UI systems are usually event driven, and so some operations become asynchronous—for example, when a window needs updating the code calls an "invalidate screen area" method which triggers a "redraw screen area" message some time later. Some very low-level operations can also be asynchronous for perform-ance reasons—for example, if the system can do I/O in parallel, it can be worth using asynchronous I/O operations (the calling code triggers a read from disk into an area of memory, but the read itself is done by a separate chunk of silicon, which notifies the main processor when the operation is complete, some time later). Similarly, if device driver code is running in an interrupt context, time-consuming processing has to be asynchronously deferred to other code so that other interrupts can be serviced quickly.

Designs involving message-passing asynchronicity usually include dia-grams that show these message flows, together with variants that illus-trate potential problems and timing windows (the slightly more formal-ized version of this is the UML sequence diagram, see subsection 3.4.2, "Diagrams").

## 3.3.3  Fault Tolerance

The first step along the road to software with six-nines reliability is to cope with failure by redundancy. This allows for *fault tolerance*—when soft-ware or hardware faults occur, there are backup systems available to take up the load. A software fault is likely to be a straightforward bug, although it might be triggered by corrupted data; a hardware fault might be the failure of a particular card in a chassis, or an entire machine in a cluster.

To deal with the consequences of a fault, it must first be detected. For software faults, this might be as simple as continuously monitoring the current set of processes reported by the operating system; for hardware faults, the detection of faults might be either a feature of the hardware, or a result of a continuous "aliveness" polling. This is heavily dependent on the physical architecture (see subsection 3.1.3, "Physical Architecture") of the software—knowing exactly where the code is supposed to run, both as processes and as processors.

Of course, the system that is used for detection of faults is itself susceptible to faults—what happens if the monitoring system goes down? To prevent an infinite regress, it's usually enough to make sure the monitoring system is as simple as possible, and as heavily tested as possible.

The overall strategy for dealing with faults depends on the prevalence of different kinds of faults. Is a hardware fault or a software fault more likely? For a hardware fault, failing over to another instance of the same hardware will normally work fine. For a software fault, there's a reasonable probability that when the backup version of the code is presented with the same inputs as the originally running primary version of the code, it will produce the same output—namely, another software fault.

In the latter case, it's entirely possible to reach a situation where a particular corrupted set of input data causes the code to bounce backwards and forwards between primary and backup instances *ad infinitum*[5]. If this is a possible or probable situation, then the fault tolerance system needs to detect this kind of situation and cope with it—ideally, by deducing what the problematic input is and removing it; more realistically, by raising an alarm for external support to look into.

Once a fault has been detected, the fault tolerance system needs to deal with the fault, by activating a backup system so that it becomes the primary instance. This might involve starting a new copy of the code, or *promoting* an already-running backup copy of the code.

The just-failed instance of the code will have state information associated with it; the newly-promoted instance of the code needs to access this state information in order to take up where the failed version left off. As such, the fault tolerance system needs a mechanism for transferring this state information.

The simplest approach for this transfer is to record the state in some external repository—perhaps a hard disk or a database. The newly-promoted code can then read back the state from this repository, and get to work. This simple approach also has the advantage that a single backup system can act as the backup for multiple primary systems—on the

---

5    At a place I used to work, this occurred on a system but the fault tolerance mechanism worked so seamlessly that the customer's only complaint was that the system was running a bit slowly.

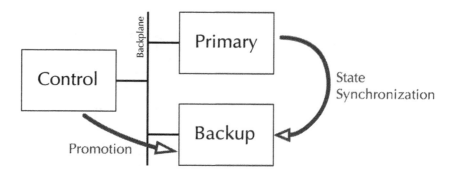

**Figure 3.3: Fault Tolerance**

assumption that only a single primary is likely to fail at a time (this setup is known as 1:N or N+1 redundancy).

There are two issues with this simple approach. The first is that the problem of a single point of failure has just been pushed to a different place—what happens if the external data repository gets a hardware fault? In practice, this is less of an issue because hardware redundancy for data stores is easily obtained (RAID disk arrays, distributed databases and so on) and because the software for performing data access is simple enough to be very reliable.

The second, more serious, issue is that the process of loading up the saved state takes time—and the time involved scales up with the amount of data involved, linearly at best. For a six-nines system, this delay as the backup instance comes up to speed is likely to endanger the all-important downtime statistics for the system.

To cope with this issue, the fault tolerance system needs a more continuous and dynamic system for transferring state to the backup instance. In a system like this, the backup instance runs all the time, and state information is continuously synchronized across from the primary to the backup; promotion from backup to primary then happens with just a flick of a switch. This approach obviously involves doubling the number of running instances, with a higher load in both processing and occupancy, but this is part of the cost of achieving high resilience (this setup is known as 1:1 or 1+1 redundancy).

Continuous, incremental updates for state information aren't enough, however. The whole fault tolerance system is necessary because the primary instance can fail at any time; it's also possible for the *backup* instance to fail. To cope with this, the state synchronization mechanism also needs a batch mode: when a new backup instance is brought on-line, it needs to acquire

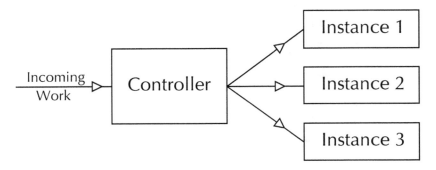

**Figure 3.4: Distributed system**

all of the current state from the primary instance to come up to speed.

The ingredients of a fault tolerance system described so far are reasonably generic. The hardware detection systems and state sychronization mechanisms can all be re-used for different pieces of software. However, each particular piece of software needs to include code that is specific to that particular code's purpose—the fault tolerance system can provide a transport for state synchronization, but the designers of each particular software product need to decide exactly what state needs to be synchronized, and when.

This set of changes to the core code to decide what to replicate (and when) isn't just a one-off, up-front cost, either. Any future enhancements and modifications to the code also need to be generated with this in mind, and tested with this in practice. The net effect is an on-going tax on development—code changes to a fault tolerant codebase are (say) 15% bigger than the equivalent changes to a non-fault tolerant codebase. For a six-nines development, this is a tax that's worth paying, but it's important to factor it into the project planning.

## 3.3.4 Distribution

A distributed processing system divides up the processing for a software system across multiple physical locations, so that the same code is running on a number of different processors. This allows the performance of the system to scale up; if the code runs properly on ten machines in parallel, then it can easily be scaled up to run on twenty machines in parallel as the traffic levels rise.

The first step on the way to distributed processing is to run multiple worker threads in parallel in the same process. This approach is very com-

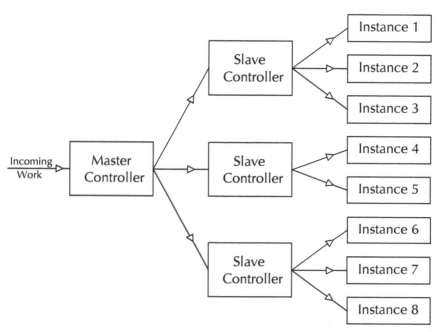

**Figure 3.5: Hierarchical distributed system**

mon and although it isn't technically a distributed system, many of the same design considerations apply.

Multiple threads allow a single process to take better advantage of a multiprocessor machine, and may improve responsiveness (if each individual chunk of work ties up a thread for a long period of time). Each thread is executing the same code, but there also needs to be some controller code that distributes the work among the various worker threads. If the individual worker threads rely on state information that is needed by other threads, then access to that data has to be correctly synchronized (see section 4.3, "Multithreading").

The next step towards distribution is to run multiple processes in parallel. Things are a little harder here, in that the memory spaces of the different processes are distinct, and so any information that needs to be shared between the processes has to be communicated between them. This could be done by putting the information into shared memory, which is effectively the same as the threading case (except that the locking primitives are different). A more flexible approach is to use a message-passing mechanism of some sort, both for triggering the individual processes to do work, and to synchronize state information among the processes.

From a message-passing, multiple process model it's a very short step to a true distributed system. Instead of the communicating between processes on the same machine, the message passing mechanism now has to communicate between different machines; instead of detecting when a worker process has terminated, the distribution mechanism now needs to detect when worker processes or processors have disappeared.

In all of these approaches, the work for the system has to be divided up among the various instances of the code. For stateless chunks of processing, this can be done in a straightforward round-robin fashion, or with an algorithm that tries to achieve more balanced processing. For processing that changes state information, it's often important to make sure that later processing for a particular transaction is performed by the same instance of the code that dealt with earlier processing.

This is easiest to do when there is a unique way of identifying a particular ongoing transaction; in this case, the identifier can be used as the input to a hashing algorithm that distributes the work in a reproducible way. However, this isn't always possible, either because there is no reliable identifier, or because the individual distributed instances of the code may come and go over time. In this case, the controller code needs more processing to keep track of the distribution of work dynamically.

As for fault tolerance, note that there is a danger of pushing the original problem back one step. For fault tolerance, where the aim is to cope with single points of failure, the system that implements failover between potential points of failure may itself become a single point of failure. For distribution, where the aim is to avoid performance bottlenecks, the system that implements the distribution may itself become a bottleneck. In practice, however, the processing performed by the distribution controller is usually much less onerous than that performed by the individual instances. If this is not the case, the system may need to become hierarchical.

## 3.3.5 Dynamic Software Upgrade

All successful software is eventually upgraded and replaced with a newer version—bugs are fixed and new functionality is included. However, there's no get-out clause for this process in a six-nines system: any downtime while the system is upgraded still counts against that maximum of thirty seconds for the year. This leads to a requirement for *dynamic software upgrade*—changing the version of the code while it's running, without inducing significant downtime.

Obviously, performing dynamic software upgrade requires a mechanism

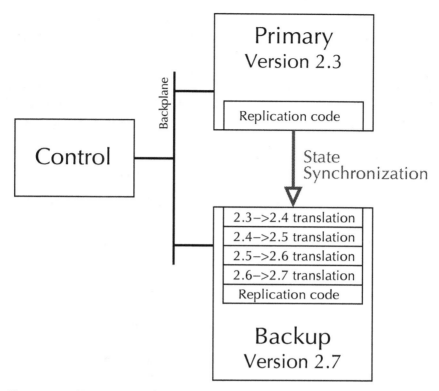

**Figure 3.6: Dynamic software update**

for reliably installing and running the new version of the code on the system. This needs some way of identifying the different versions of the code that are available, and connecting to the right version. This also depends on the physical architecture (see subsection 3.1.3, "Physical Architecture") of the code: how the code is split up into distinct executables, shared libraries and configuration files affects the granularity of the upgrade.

A simple example of this upgrade mechanism is the one used for shared libraries on UNIX systems—there might be several versions of the raw code, stored in versioned files (libc.so.2.2, libc.so.2.3, libc.so.3.0, libc.so.3.1), with symbolic links which indicate the currently active versions (libc.so.2->libc.so.2.2, libc.so.3->libc.so.3.1, libc.so->libc.so.3) and which can be instantly swapped between versions. This mechanism needs to go both ways—sadly, it's common to have to downgrade from a new version to go back to the drawing board.

However, the difficult part of dynamic software upgrade is not the substitution of the new code for the old code. What is much more difficult is ensuring that the active state for the running old system gets transferred across to the new version.

To a first approximation, this is the same problem as for fault tolerance (see subsection 3.3.3, "Fault Tolerance"), and a normal way to implement dynamic software upgrade is to leverage an existing fault tolerant system:

- With a primary instance and backup instance both running version 1.0, bring down the backup instance.
- Upgrade the backup instance to version 1.1.
- Bring the backup instance back online, and wait for state synchronization to complete.
- Explicitly force a failover from the version 1.0 primary instance to the version 1.1 backup instance.
- If the new version 1.1 primary instance is working correctly, upgrade the now-backup version 1.0 instance to also run version 1.1 of the code.
- Bring the second instance of version 1.1 online as the new backup.

As with fault tolerance, the mechanisms for dynamic software upgrade can be shared among different software products, but the internal semantics of the state synchronization process have to be designed as part of each specific software product. This is a more difficult problem than for fault tolerance, though: for each set of state information, there may need to be a translation process between the old and new versions of the information (in both directions, to allow for downgrading as well as upgrading). Ideally, the translation process should also be "stackable"—if a system needs to be upgraded from version 2.3 to version 2.7, downtime is kept to a minimum if this can be done in one step rather than via versions 2.4, 2.5 and 2.6.

In practice, this means that any new state information that is added to later versions of the code needs to have a default value and behaviour, to cope with state that's been dynamically updated from an earlier version of the code. What's more, the designers of the new feature need to make and implement decisions about what should happen if state that relies on the new feature gets downgraded. In worst-case scenarios, this migration of state may be so difficult that it's not sensible to implement it—the consequences of the resulting downtime may be less than the costs of writing huge amounts of translation code.

Again (as with fault tolerance), the inclusion of dynamic software upgrade functionality imposes a serious development tax on all future changes to the product's codebase. Each bug fix and feature enhancement has to be carefully examined and tested in comparison with a matrix of earlier versions of the product, to ensure that state migration can be performed.

# 3.4 Communicating the Design

## 3.4.1 Why and Who

It's not enough to have a design. That design needs to be communicated to all of the people who are involved in the project, both present and future.

The mere fact of attempting to communicate the design to someone else is a great smoke test for spotting holes in the design. If you can't be successfully explain it to a bright colleague, the chances are that you don't fully understand it yourself.

For a larger system, the design process may well occur in layers. The overall architecture gets refined into a high-level design, whose components are each in turn subject to a low-level design, and then each of the low-level designs gets turned into code. This is the implementation process: each abstract layer is implemented in terms of a lower-level, more concrete layer.

At each stage of this process, the people who are responsible for this implementation process need to understand the design. The chances are that there is more than a single implementer, and that the sum of all of designs in all of the layer is more than will fit in a single implementer's head.

Therefore the clearer the communication of each layer of the design, the greater chance there is that the next layer down will be implemented well. If one layer is well explained, documented and communicated, the layer below is much more likely to work well and consistently with the rest of the design.

The intended audience for the communication of the design is not just these different layers of implementers of the design. In the future, the code is likely to be supported, maintained and enhanced, and all of the folk who do these tasks can be well assisted by understanding the guiding principles behind the original design.

## 3.4.2  Diagrams

One of the most powerful tools in discussing and communicating a design is a diagram. Many people think visually; a simple diagram of blocks and lines can help to visualize the design and make it clear. For asynchronous systems (see subsection 3.3.2, "Asynchronicity"), explicitly including the flow of time as an axis in a diagram can help to illuminate potential timing problems.

This isn't news; in fact, it's so well known that there is an entire standardized system for depicting software systems and their constituents: the Unified Modeling Language (UML). Having a standard system can obviously save time during design discussions, but an arbitrary boxes-and-lines picture is usually clear enough for most purposes.

Colour can also help when communicating a design diagram—to differentiate between different types of component, or to indicate differing options for the design[6].

## 3.4.3  Documentation

Documenting the design is important because it allows the intent behind the design to be communicated even to developers who aren't around at the time of the original design. It also allows the higher-level concepts behind the design to be explained without getting bogged down in too many details.

In recent years, many software engineers have begun to include documentation hooks in their source code. A variety of tools (from Doxygen to JavaDoc all the way back to the granddaddy of them all, Donald Knuth's WEB system) can then mechanically extract interface documentation and so on.

Any documentation is better than nothing, but it's important not to confuse this sort of thing with real documentation. Book publishers like O'Reilly sell many books that describe software systems for which the source code is freely available—even when that source code includes this kind of documentation hooks. These books are organized and structured to explain the code without getting bogged down in details; they cover the concepts involved, they highlight key scenarios, they include pictures, and they're still useful even when the software has moved on several versions since the book was published. In other words, they are roughly equivalent

---

6    Note that I got all the way through this section without repeating the old adage about a picture being worth a thousand words. Until just now, of course.

to a good design document.

Some points to bear in mind when generating design documents:

- Structure: The text should be well-structured, in order to make it easy to read and review—software developers tend to think about things in a structured way.
- Rationale: As well as describing *how* the code is supposed to work, the design document should also describe *why* it has been designed that way. In fact, it's often useful to discuss other potential approaches and explain why they have *not* been taken—people often learn from and remember (potential) horror stories. This helps future developers understand what kinds of changes to the design are likely to work, and which are likely to cause unintended consequences.
- Satisfaction of the requirements: It should be clear from the documentation of the design that the requirements for the software are actually satisfied by the design. In particular, it's often worth including a section in the design that revisits any requirements use cases (see section 2.2, "Use Cases"), showing how the internals of the code would work in those scenarios—many people understand things better as a result of induction (seeing several examples and spotting the patterns involved) than deduction (explaining the code's behaviour and its direct consequences).
- Avoidance of the passive voice: The design document describes how things get done. The previous sentence uses the passive voice: "things get done" avoids the question of exactly who or what does things. For a design document to be unambiguous, it should describe exactly which chunk of code performs all of the functionality described.

# 4 CODE

This chapter deals with the code itself. This is a shorter chapter than some, because I've tried to avoid repeating too much of the standard advice about how to write good code on a line-by-line basis—in fact, many of the topics of this chapter are really aspects of low-level design rather than pure coding[1]. However, there are still a few things that are rarely explored and which can be particularly relevant when the aim is to achieve the highest levels of quality.

## 4.1 Portability

Writing portable code encourages good design and good code. To write portable code, the developers have to understand both the problem domain and the solution domain, and what the boundary between the two is. It's very useful from a business perspective too: portable code can be sold on a variety of different platforms, without being locked into a particular operating system or database vendor. Portability is planning for medium term and long term success; it assumes that the lifetime of the software is going to be longer than the popularity of the current platforms[2].

There are different levels of portability, depending on how much functionality is assumed to be provided by the environment. This might be as little as a C compiler and a standard C library—or perhaps not even that, given the limitations of some embedded systems (for example, no floating point support). It might be a set of functionality that corresponds to some

---

1  But having "High-Level Design" and "Low-Level Design" chapters isn't as neat as "Design" and "Code".

2  Some of the first software I ever worked on (in 1987) is still being sold today, having run on mainframes, minicomputers, dedicated terminals, large UNIX systems and even Windows and Linux systems.

defined or de facto standard, such as the various incarnations of UNIX. For the software to actually *do* something, there has to be some kind of assumption about the functionality provided by the environment—perhaps the availability of a reliable database system, or a standard sockets stack.

It's sensible to encapsulate the interactions between the product code and the environment. Encapsulation is always a good idea, but in this case it gives a definitive description of the functionality required from the environment. That way, if and when the software is moved to a different environment, it's easier to adapt—hopefully by mapping the new environment to the encapsulated interface, but sometimes by changing the interface slightly and adapting the product code too.

For six-nines software, the interactions between the product code and the environment are often very low-level. Many of these interfaces are standardized—the C library, a sockets library, the POSIX thread library—but they can also be very environment specific; for example, notification mechanisms for hardware failures or back-plane communication mechanisms. Some of these low-level interfaces can be very unusual for programmers who are used to higher level languages. For example, some network processors have two different types of memory: general-purpose memory for control information, and packet buffers for transporting network data. The packet buffers are optimized for moving a whole set of data through the system quickly, but at the expense of making access to individual bytes in a packet slower and more awkward. Taken together, this means that software that may need to be ported to these systems has to carefully distinguish between the two different types of memory.

All of these interfaces between the software and its environment need to be encapsulated, and in generating these encapsulations it's worth examining more systems than just the target range of portability. For example, when generating an encapsulated interface to a sockets stack for a UNIX-based system, it's worth checking how the Windows implementation of sockets would fit under the interface. Likewise, when encapsulating the interface to a database system, it's worth considering a number of potential underlying databases—Oracle, MySQL, DB2, PostgreSQL, etc.—to see whether a small amount of extra effort in the interface would encapsulate a much wider range of underlying implementations (see subsection 3.1.2, "Black Box Principle"). As ever, it's a balance between an interface that's a least common denominator that pushes lots of processing up to the product code, and an interface that relies so closely on one vendor's special features that the product code is effectively locked into that vendor forever.

# 4.2  Internationalization

Internationalization is the process of ensuring that software can run successfully in a variety of different locales. Locales involve more than just the language used in the user interface; different cultures have different conventions for displaying various kinds of data. For example, 5/6/07 would be interpreted as the 5th June 2007 in the UK, but as 6th May 2007 in the US. Ten billion[3] would be written 10,000,000,000 in the US, but as 10,00,00,00,000 in India.

Once software has been internationalized, it can then be *localized*[4] by supplying all of the locale-specific settings for a particular target: translated user interface texts, date and time settings, currency settings and so on.

As with portability, writing internationalized code is planning ahead for success (in markets outside of the original country of distribution). More immediately, thinking about internationalization encourages better design and code, because it forces the designer to think carefully about the concepts behind some common types of data. Some examples will help to make this clearer.

What exactly is a string? Is it conceptually a sequence of bytes or a sequence of characters? If you have to iterate through that sequence, this distinction makes a huge difference. To convert from a concrete sequence of bytes to a logical sequence of characters (or vice versa), the code needs to know the *encoding*: UTF-8 or ISO-Latin-1 or UCS-2 etc. To convert from a logical sequence of characters to human-readable text on screen, the code needs to have a *glyph* for every character, which depends on the fonts available for display.

What exactly is a date and time? Is it in some local timezone, or in a fixed well-known timezone? If it's in a local timezone, does the code incorrectly assume that there are 24 hours in a day or that time always increases (neither assumption is true during daylight-saving time shifts)? If it's stored in a fixed timezone like UTC[5], does the code need to convert it to and from a more friendly local time for the end user? If so, where does the information needed for the conversion come from and what happens

---

3  Ten *US* billions, that is. Traditional UK billions are a thousand times larger than US billions—a million millions rather than a thousand millions.

4  Internationalization and localization are often referred to as I18N and L10N for the hard-of-typing—the embedded number indicates how many letters have been skipped.

5  Coordinated Universal Time, the modern name for Greenwich Mean Time (GMT). Also known as Zulu time (Z).

when it changes[6]?

What's in a name? Dividing a person's name into "first name" and "last name" isn't appropriate for many Asian countries, where typical usage has a family name first, followed by a given name. Even with the more useful division into "given name" and "family name", there are still potential wrinkles: many cultures have gender-specific variants of names, so a brother and sister would not have matching family names. Icelandic directories are organized by given name rather than "family name", because Iceland uses a patronymic system (where the "family name" is the father's name followed by "-son" or "-dottir")—brothers share a family name, but father and son do not.

Being aware of the range of different cultural norms for various kinds of data makes it much more likely that the code will accurately and robustly model the core concepts involved.

## 4.3 Multithreading

This section concentrates on one specific area of low-level design and coding that can have significant effects on quality: multithreading.

In multithreaded code, multiple threads of execution share access to the same set of memory areas, and they have to ensure that access to that memory is correctly synchronized to prevent corruption of data. Exactly the same considerations apply when multiple processes use explicitly shared memory, although in practice there are fewer problems because access to the shared area is more explicit and deliberate.

Multithreaded code is much harder to write correctly than single-threaded code, a fact which is not typically appreciated by new programmers. It's easy to neglect to fully mutex-protect all areas of data, with no apparent ill effects for the first few thousand times the code is run. Even if all the data is properly protected, it still possible to encounter more subtle deadlock problems induced by inverted locking hierarchies.

Of course, it is possible to design and code around these difficulties successfully. However, the only way to continue being successful as the size of the software scales up is by imposing some serious discipline on coding practices—rigorously checked conventions on mutex protection for data areas, wrapped locking calls to allow checks for locking hierarchy inversions, well-defined conventions for thread entrypoints and so on.

Even with this level of discipline, multithreading still imposes some

---

6   Such as in August 2005, when the US Congress moved the dates for daylight-saving from 2007.

serious costs to maintainability. The key aspect of this is *unpredictability*—multithreaded code devolves the responsibility for scheduling different parts of the code to the operating system, and there is no reliable way of determining in what order different parts of the code will run. This makes it very difficult to build reliable regression tests that exercise the code fully; it also means that when bugs do occur, they are *much* harder to debug (see section 6.6, "Debugging").

So when do the benefits of multithreading outweigh the costs? When is worth using multithreading?

- When there is little or no interaction between different threads. The most common pattern for this is when there are several worker threads that execute the same code path, but that code path includes blocking operations. In this case, the multithreading is essential for the code to perform responsively enough, but the design is effectively single threaded: if the code only ran one thread, it would behave exactly the same (only slower).
- When there are processing-intensive operations that need to be performed. In this case, the most straightforward design may be for the heavy processing to be done in a synchronous way by a dedicated thread, while other threads continue with the other functions of the software and wait for the processing to complete (thus ensuring UI responsiveness, for example).
- When you have to. Sometimes an essential underlying API requires multithreading; this is most common in UI frameworks.

## 4.4  Coding Standards

Everyone has their own favourite coding convention, and they usually provide explanations of what the benefits of their particular preferences are. These preferences vary widely depending on the programming language and development environment; however, it's worth stepping back to explore what the benefits are for the whole concept of coding standards.

The first benefit of a common set of conventions across a codebase is that it helps with maintainability. When a developer explores a new area of code, it's in a format that they're familiar with, and so it's ever so slightly easier to read and understand. Standard naming conventions for different types of variables—local, global, object members—can make the intent of a piece of code clearer to the reader.

The next benefit is that it can sometimes help to avoid common errors, by encoding wisdom learnt in previous developments. For example, in C-like languages it's often recommended that comparison operations should be written as if (12 == var) rather than if (var == 12), to avoid the possibility of mistyping and getting if (var = 12) instead. Another example is that coding standards for portable software often ban the use of C/C++ unions, since their layout in memory is very implementation-dependent. For portable software (see section 4.1, "Portability") that has to deal with byte flipping issues, a variable naming convention that indicates the byte ordering can save many bugs[7].

With these kinds of recommendations, it's important that the coding standards include a description of the *reasons* for the recommendations. Sometimes it becomes necessary to break particular recommendations, and this can only be done in a sensible way if the developers know whether a particular provision is just for tidiness or is to avoid a particular compiler problem (say).

An often-overlooked benefit of a consistent coding convention is that it can make the source code easier to analyse and process. Fully parsing a high-level programming language is non-trivial (especially for something as complicated as C++); however, if the coding standards impose some additional structure, it's often possible to get useful information with more trivial tools (such as scripts written in awk or Perl). For example, I've generated code coverage information for a Linux kernel module by running the source code through an awk script that replaced particular instances of { with a trace statement (something like {{static int hit=0; if (!hit) {TRACE("hit %s:%d", __FILE__, __LINE__); hit=1;}}). The generated trace information was then post-processed by other simple scripts to generate reasonably accurate line coverage data. For this example, the scripts were only tractable because the source code structure was predictable.

Finally, there can occasionally be a trivial benefit if the source code gets delivered to customers: it looks more professional. Obviously, this more style than substance, but it can help to reinforce the impression that the developers have put care and attention into the source code.

Given a coding convention, it's important not to waste the time of the developers with the business of policing that coding convention. Most provisions of the coding standard can and should be checked mechanically—when new code is checked into the codebase, and as part of the regular build process (see subsection 4.6.3, "Enforcing Standards").

---

7   For example, if an h or n prefix indicates ordering, then it's easy to spot that hSeqNum = packet->nLastSeqNum + 1; is probably wrong.

# 4.5 Tracing

Tracing is the addition of extra diagnostic statements to the code to emit useful information about the state of the processing being performed. In its simplest form, this can just involve scattering a few choice `if (verbose) fprintf(stderr, "reached here")` lines throughout the code. In this section, we describe a much more comprehensive approach to the same basic technique.

In application software, developers usually solve problems by stepping through the code in a debugger. Examining the output from internal trace in the code is equivalent to this process, but it has a few advantages compared to the debugger.

- Tracing is available and accessible on systems that don't have a debugger or where using a debugger is awkward (for example, embedded systems or low-level device drivers).
- Trace output will be the same on different environments, so there's no need to learn about the foibles of different debuggers.
- Trace output covers a whole sequence of processing, rather than just the processing occurring at a particular point in time. This means it's possible to step backwards in the code as well as forwards, without having to re-run the scenario (which is particularly helpful for intermittent bugs).

Tracing is not unique to higher quality software development, but it is generally implemented more thoroughly in these kinds of software. Higher reliability correlates with more efficient debugging, which correlates with better internal diagnostics.

In some respects, trace statements in the code are similar to comments—they both consist of text destined for human readers, closely linked with particular chunks of code. However, tracing has a slightly different purpose than comments; trace statements indicate *what* the code is doing, whereas comments explain *why* the code is doing it (and of course the code itself is *how* it's doing it). As a result, trace statements often indicate trivial things that would be pointless if they were comments instead—processing has reached this branch, this variable has been set to that value, and so on.

Trace statements explain what the code is doing as it does it, in order to allow analysis and debugging of the code. Bearing this in mind, there are a few rules of thumb for the developers which will help to maximize the usefulness of the trace:

- It's a good idea to have a coding standard that requires a trace statement in every branch of the code. If this is enforced, then the complete path of the flow of processing through the code can be reliably retraced. (This has the side benefit that code coverage information can be derived from the tracing even when the toolchain doesn't support coverage.)

- Make sure that trace statements contain as much useful information as possible. It's easy to fall into a habit of inserting trace statements that just say "got to this line of code" (particularly if the previous suggestion is enforced on developers who don't understand the value of tracing); it's much more helpful when the values of key variables are included in the trace.
- Given the previous suggestion, the tracing system should cope with the inclusion of arbitrary pieces of information—say by allowing C `printf`-like formatting, or use of C++ overloaded `operator<<`.
- To make sure the developers understand the value of tracing in general, and tracing extra parameters in particular, it's worth insisting that they try debugging a few problems just using tracing and other diagnostics, with no access to a debugger.

There are possible penalties to including tracing in the code, and it's important that the tracing framework avoids these penalties where possible.

The most obvious penalty is performance—particularly if every possible branch of the code includes a trace statement (as suggested above). However, this is easily dealt with by allowing the trace framework to be compiled out—a release build can be mechanically preprocessed to remove the trace statements.

Another penalty with the inclusion of copious quantities of trace is that it becomes more difficult to see the wood for the trees. Key events get lost in the morass of trace output, disk files fill up, and trace from perfectly-working areas of code obscures the details from the problem areas. Again, it's not difficult to build a trace framework in a way that alleviates these problems.

- Include enough information in the trace data to allow filtering in or out for particular areas of code. A simple but effective mechanism in C or C++ is to quietly include the `__FILE__` and `__LINE__` information in the tracing system. This immediately allows trace from particular files to be included or excluded; if the codebase has an appropriate file naming convention, this mechanism can also work on a component by component basis (for example, filter in trace from any source code named `xyz_*`). The filtering setup can be set from a configuration file, or (ideally) modified while the code is actually running.

- For code that deals with many similar things in parallel, make sure the trace system will include enough context in its output—and again, allow filtering on this information. This context information might be a unique identifier for a key database record, or the address of an essential object or control block.
- Use different levels of tracing, where significant events show up at a higher level than step-by-step trace statements. For example: code branch tracing < function entry/exit tracing < internal interface tracing < external interface tracing. The trace framework can then allow for these different levels of trace to be compiled in and out separately, and filtered in or out separately (in other words, there is a compile-time trace level and a run-time trace level).
- Include mechanisms to trace out the entire contents of activities on external interfaces (so for a message driven system, this would mean saving the whole contents of the message). If the code is deterministic, then this makes it possible to regenerate the behaviour of the code—re-running the external interface trace provides exactly the same inputs, so the code will generate exactly the same outputs.
- Include mechanisms to limit the amount of trace information generated. If tracing goes to file, this can be as simple as alternating between a pair of files with a maximum size for each file. A more sophisticated system might trace to an internal buffer, which is only written out to disk as a result of particular triggers (for example, when the developer triggers it, or when a SEGV signal is caught).

With a reliable and comprehensive trace system in place, it soon become possible to use that system for all sorts of additional purposes:

- If tracing is ubiquitous in the code, it's possible to generate code coverage information even in environments whose toolchain doesn't support it. No changes to the code are needed—just some scripting and/or tweaks to the trace system to track which trace lines have been hit.
- Similarly, it's possible to get some quick and dirty identification of the most frequently executed code in the product, by adding counters to the trace system.
- If every function traces entry and exit in a standard way, the tracing system can be used to give call stacks when the operating system doesn't.

The following example should help to give a flavour of what code that includes tracing could look like.

```
#include <cpptrace.h>
```

```cpp
#include <Fred.h>

void Fred::doSomething(int a)
{
  TRACE_FN("doSomething");

  TRC_DBG("called with "<<a);
  if (a==0) {
    TRC_NRM("zero case, mOtherField="<<mOtherField);
    doOtherThing(&a);
  } else {
    TRC_NRM("non-zero, use mField = "<<mField);
    doOtherThing(&mField);
  }
}
```

For this particular C++ example:

- The TRACE_FN invocation generates entry and exit trace for the function. It is implemented by including an object on the stack whose constructor generates the entry trace and whose destructor generates the exit trace. As such, the exit trace is generated even when the function is terminated by a C++ exception.
- The trace invocations are all macros that can be compiled out.
- The contents of each trace invocation use C++ operator<<, so arbitrary types can be traced.

The output of this code might look something like the following.

```
2006-03-21 14:36:05 224:b2a4 Fred.cpp::doSomething  6 { Entry
2006-03-21 14:36:05 224:b2a4 Fred.cpp::doSomething  8 _ called with 0
2006-03-21 14:36:05 224:b2a4 Fred.cpp::doSomething 10 . zero case, mOtherField=/tmp/file
2006-03-21 14:36:05 224:b2a4 Fred.cpp::doSomething  0 } Exit
```

This trace output includes the following information, in a fixed format which is easy to filter after the fact.

- Date and time the trace was generated.
- Process and thread ID that generated the trace.
- Module containing the code.
- Method name (set up by the TRACE_FN call).
- Line number.
- Trace level indicator. This includes { and } for function entry and exit, which means that the bracket matching features of editors can be used to jump past particular functions.
- The trace message itself, including any additional data traced out.

Although the title of this section is "Tracing", similar considerations apply to logging as well. The key distinction between tracing and logging is that tracing is purely aimed at the developers of the code, whereas logging involves emitting information that is of use to future administrators of the running product. This distinction does mean that there are a couple of key differences between the two, though.

- Tracing is typically compiled out of the final released product, but logging is not (and so should be checked to confirm that it doesn't involve a significant performance penalty).
- Logging messages should be normally be internationalized so that the product can be localized for different nationalities of administrators, whereas tracing messages can be fixed in the language of the development team.

# 4.6  Managing the Codebase

During the coding phase of a project, the developers also need to deal with all of the ancillary bits and pieces that are needed to convert the source code into binaries, get those binaries running on the desired systems, and keep track of what binaries are running where.

## 4.6.1  Revision Control

The first step of this process is to make sure that the source code itself is available and safe from screw-ups. The latter of these equates to making sure that there's a reliable source code control system, and that it gets backed up frequently.

A source code control system can actually cover a number of different areas, all related to the primary goal of keeping track of versions of source code files:

- For individual developers, it can be useful to keep track of different versions of files as they are under development. For this kind of source control:
    - Different revisions will only be hours or minutes apart.
    - Old revisions will only ever be re-visited by the developer themselves, and then only within a few days of their creation.
    - Revisions need not be complete, coherent or compilable.
- For the project team as a whole, the main revision control system keeps the current tip version of the entire source code. For this:
    - Different revisions will typically be days or weeks apart.
    - Files will be created and modified by a variety of different team members.
    - Each revision is normally expected to be a working version of the file, that compiles cleanly and can be used by other members of the team. This can sometimes be checked mechanically—files

that don't compile or that fail automated checks against coding standards (see section 4.4, "Coding Standards") are rejected.

- It's common to check in a collection of related files at once, and the revision system needs to allow that entire set of changes to be retrieved as a unit (for example, so that a vital fix can be merged and back-applied to a different codebase).
- Changes to the master tip version of the source code are often correlated with other tracking systems—most commonly with a bug tracking system (see subsection 4.6.2, "Other Tracking Systems").

- When the project hits the outside world, a release control system is needed. This correlates between the delivered binary files that are run by customers, and the source code files that were used to create those binaries. For this:
  - New releases will typically be weeks or (more likely) months apart.
  - It should be easy to extract an entire codebase which corresponds to a particular released binary (for tracking down bugs in that released binary)
  - It must be possible to branch the revision tree. This allows some-but-not-all of the changes in the current tip revision to be back-applied, so that important bug fixes can be included in a new set of released binary files without including other potentially destabilizing changes.
  - For convenience, it's sometimes worth revision-tracking the binary files as well as the source code files.
  - For a completely bulletproof system, it can be worth version-tracking the entire toolchain (compiler, linker, system include files and so on) to make sure that a previous version can be regenerated in a way that is byte-for-byte identical to the original release.

There are many version control systems to choose from; the primary deciding factor for that choice is reliability, but almost all systems are completely reliable. That leaves extra features as the next factor on which to base a choice—but in practice, most extra features can built onto a basic system with some scripting, provided that the system allows scripts to be wrapped around it. The net of this is that it's often easiest to stick with a known system that the developers have experience of (see subsection 3.2.5, "Avoiding the Cutting Edge").

## 4.6.2  Other Tracking Systems

As well as tracking changes to the source code, software projects usually need to track a variety of other pieces of information. These other pieces of information may well be more relevant to other stages in the lifecycle of a project—such as testing (see chapter 6, "Test") or support (see chapter 7, "Support")—but since the source code is the heart of a software project, it makes sense to consider all the related tracking systems together.

The most important information to track is the *reasons* for changes to the source code. Depending on the phase of the project, there are a variety of potential reasons why the source code might change:

- Development: writing the original version of the code in the first place.
- Changes from reviews: design reviews and code reviews are likely to result in a number of changes to existing code.
- Enhancements: additional features and functionality for the software requires code changes to implement it.
- Changes from testing: the various test phases (see chapter 6, "Test") will expose problems in the code that need to be fixed. This is a subset of "Bugs" below.
- Bugs: problems in the code that have been exposed by testing or reported by customers and users induce changes in the source code to correct those problems.

Of these categories, bugs are by far the most numerous, so it is common practice to use a bug system to track *all* changes to the code. With this setup, specific bug categories ("development" or "enhancement") can be used to track code changes that do not originate from problems in the code.

The bug tracking system needs to be closely tied to the revision control system, correlating code changes against bugs and also correlating bugs against code changes.

- For a change to the code, the revision control system needs to indicate which bug the change was for. If a future bug involves that area of code, the information in the bug tracking system elucidates the reasons why the code is there, and what might be the potential consequences of changing it. In other words, this allows the developer to check whether a new change to the code is re-introducing an old bug.
- For a bug, the bug tracking system needs to indicate the set of source

code changes that correspond to its fix[8]. If a bug recurs or is incompletely fixed, this record allows the developers to determine if the fix has been altered or if it should apply to other areas of the code.

For smaller codebases, it can also be helpful to automatically generate a combined summary report that lists (by date) the files in the codebase that have changed, together with the corresponding bug number. This report shows the codebase activity at a glance, so it's easier to figure out underlying causes when things go awry. When things mysteriously stop working, it's usually a recent change that's to blame—even if it's in an apparently unrelated area.

Similarly, it's also useful to have a mechanical way of generating a list of all of the changes between particular dates or releases, as a collection of both affected files and affected bugs. This can show the areas where testing should be concentrated for a new release, or the code changes that should be re-examined in case of a regression between releases.

Once software escapes into the wild and is used by real users, it is sadly common for them to lose track of exactly what software they have. The support process is much harder if you don't know exactly what code you're supporting, so it's often helpful to add systems that make identification of code versions more automatic and reliable.

- Embed version numbers for each source code file into the corresponding binary file. Most version control systems include a facility to automatically expand a keyword into the version number (for example `$Id: mycode.cpp,v 1.129 2007/02/20 14:06:19 dmd$` for RCS). This can then be embedded in a string (`static const char rcsid[] = "$Id: mycode.cpp,v 1.129 2007/02/20 14:06:19 dmd $";`) that is easy to extract from the built binaries (using UNIX `ident`, for example).

- Embed release identification into the product as a whole. It should be easy for customers to figure out which version of the product they are running; for products with a UI, it is normal for a "Help, About" box to display the overall product identification string.

- Ensure that release numbers are always unique. Sometimes bugs are spotted mere moments after a new version of a product is released; avoid the temptation to nip in a fix and re-use the same version number.

- It can also be helpful to embed build information into the released product, identifying the date and time and build options used. The

---

8   If the codebase has a regressible system of test harnesses, the bug record should also indicate which test cases display the bug.

date and time of the build can be included in the overall product version identification to guarantee the uniqueness described in the previous bullet.

## 4.6.3  Enforcing Standards

A previous section (see section 4.4, "Coding Standards") discussed the rationale behind project or company wide coding standards. However, just relying on the developers themselves to comply with these standards is rarely enough—they need to be checked mechanically instead. These mechanical checks are typically implemented in some sort of scripting language—perhaps awk, Perl or Python.

There are three common times to run the checks.

* By hand, for individual developers who want to check the current state of compliance for the code that they are working on.
* During the code check-in process, to make sure that code that doesn't comply with the relevant standards doesn't make it into the codebase.
* During the regular code build process, to catch any problems that have slipped in.

Sadly, in the real world there are always going to be exceptions to the standards—perhaps an imported set of code files that conform to a different standard, or an OS-specific module that doesn't need to conform to the same portability requirements. As such, it's important that the systems for checking standards compliance include a way of allowing agreed exceptions.

## 4.6.4  Building the Code

Customers for a software product normally don't just get the source code. Instead, they get a set of binary files that have been built from the source code, together with a variety of other files (help files, documentation, localization files, default configuration files etc.). To produce the binary files from the source code, still more files are needed—makefiles, build jobs, install image creation scripts, tools to extract documentation, and so on.

The same considerations that apply to source code files apply to all of these ancillary files, but for some reason this seems to happen much more rarely. Common sections of build jobs should be commonized rather than copied and pasted, so that fixing a problem in the build only has to be done in one place—the same as for code. The auxiliary files should all be stored under revision control, and backed up, so that bad changes can be reverted—the same as for code. Files shouldn't generate excessive numbers of benign warning messages that might obscure real error messages—the same as for code.

To make it less likely that developers will break the build, it's useful if they can easily run their own local version of the build to confirm the state of any code they're about to check in. This means that the build should be easy to run from beginning to end, preferably with a single command, and it should ideally have reliable dependency checking so that only code that has changed gets rebuilt—in a large codebase, anything else is tempting the developers to cut corners.

The build system should also build everything that the customers are going to get, not just the raw binaries—which might mean that the end result of the build is a self-extracting archive that includes help files and localization files and so on.

The build system can also generate things that customers are not going to get—notably the internal test harnesses for the product, and the results of running those test harnesses. This gives a much higher confidence level for the current state of the code than just whether it compiles and links or not.

As the size of the team and the project scales up, it also becomes worth investing the time to automate various build-related activities. This might start with a system to automatically filter out known benign warning messages from the build; with a larger codebase, there might be a system to automatically email build output for particular components to the component owners. For a more established, stable codebase, it's often worth building a system that emails any new build problems to the developer that most recently touched the codebase or the relevant file.

## 4.6.5  Delivering the Code

The final stage of the code's journey is its delivery to the customer. Once the binaries are built, some mechanism is needed to ensure that the code ends up running correctly on the destination machine. This is particularly important for software that will be installed by end-users, but even deliveries to other software engineering groups require some planning and coordination.

Building installers is harder than many developers realize. What seems like a simple matter of moving files between disks is much more complicated when all of the potential factors are considered. To get the code running correctly on the destination machine, the install process needs to consider:

- Is this the right destination machine? Is the operating system a supported version? Are all of the required libraries already installed? Is there enough disk space? Are all the hardware requirements satisfied?
- Is this the right code? Are there earlier versions of the code installed? If there are, does the new version replace or live alongside the existing version? If there aren't, can a patch install still proceed? Is this the build variant that matches the local configuration?
- Does the code run? Does it rely on being installed into a particular place? Does it rely on being installed with particular permission levels? Does it have necessary access to the network or the Internet?
- Does the code run *correctly*? Are there self-tests that can be run? Are there diagnostics that can be gathered and reported to help locate problems?

Rather than deferring all of these issues to the end of the software development cycle, it's often best to build install packages as part of the regular build system. With this approach, the install packages are built and used regularly throughout the development cycle, increasing the chances of spotting problems with the installer.

# 5  CODE REVIEW

Code reviews are a very effective tool for improving the quality of both the software itself and the developers that produce the software. When they're done badly, code reviews can also be a pointless exercise in box-ticking that wastes time and annoys developers. This chapter discusses the how and why of code reviews in a level of detail that is rarely covered, in order to help them lean towards the former rather than the latter.

## 5.1  Rationale: Why do code reviews?

So what's the point of code reviews? Even among folk who agree that they're a good idea, the full rationale behind code reviews is rarely examined in detail.

### 5.1.1  Correctness

The most obvious idea behind a code review is to try to find bugs. It's well known that the earlier a bug is found, the cheaper it is to fix—and a code review is the earliest possible time after the code has been written that this can happen (other than not putting in bugs in the first place).

A second pair of eyes examining the code is a useful sanity check to catch bugs. If the reviewer has more experience with the technologies involved (from programming language to underlying APIs to operating system to programming methodology), then they may well know "gotchas" to watch out for.

Interestingly, this aspect of code reviewing becomes much less important when all of the parties involved are experienced and know their stuff. In this sort of situation, the number of straightforward logic bugs spotted at code review drops to an almost negligible number—at which point the other factors below come into their own. At this stage, thorough and cunning testing is a much more efficient way to eke out the remaining bugs.

However, even in a halcyon situation where everyone involved is experienced and skilled, there is still the opportunity for integration bugs, and this is worth bearing in mind when assigning code reviewers. This is particularly true of new development—if new component A uses new component B, then the coder of component B may well be a good candidate to review the code for component A (and vice versa). Regardless of how thorough and well-written the interface specifications are, there may be ambiguities that slip through.

## 5.1.2 Maintainability

The most valuable reason for a code review is to ensure the maintainability of the code. Maintainability is all about making it easy for future developers to understand, debug, fix and enhance the code, which in turn relies on them being able to correctly understand the code as it stands today.

The code review is an ideal place for a dry run for this process. The original coder *can't* judge whether the code is easy or difficult for someone else to understand, so the code reviewer is in a much better position to judge this. To put it another way, the code reviewer is the first of potentially dozens of people who will have to make sense of the code in the future—and so an effective code review can make a lot of difference.

To understand how much difference this can make, consider the conditions under which bugs from the field get fixed. Particularly if it's an urgent problem, the developer fixing the problem may be under time pressure, short on sleep, and generally in the worst possible mood for appreciating some incredibly cunning but incomprehensible code. Anything which eases the understanding of the code in this situation hugely increases the chances of getting a quick, correct fix instead of a quick hack that causes several more problems later on. This is difficult to measure with short term metrics (such as lines of code written per developer-day), but does show up in longer term bug rates and support costs—and in the more intangible aspect of developer morale.

Stepping back, the most important aspect of maintainability is good design, which should hopefully already be in place well before the code review takes place. Once that design is in place, maintainability is all about *communication*—communicating the intent of that design and of the lower-level details of the code—and the code review is an ideal time to test out that communication.

## 5.1.3 Education

An often overlooked aspect to code reviews is that they help to educate the developers involved—to develop the developers, as it were.

The most obvious side of this is that the reviewer gets educated about the details and layout of the specific code being reviewed. This means there are *two* people who understand the code in detail, which gives more depth in the team for situations where the original author isn't available (they're on holiday, or they've left the team, or they've been run over by a bus).

This can help to persuade those developers who bristle at the thought of someone else criticising their perfect code: spreading the knowledge around means they won't have to support the code forever.

Longer term, it's also a good way for developers to educate each other. The reviewer can see or suggest alternative ways of coding things, whether neat tricks or minor performance tweaks. A more experienced reviewer can use code reviews to train a junior programmer; a junior reviewer can use the review as an opportunity to ask questions about why things were done in particular ways. For example, a junior C++ programmer might ask why all of the loops in the code have ++ii instead of ii++, at which point the more experienced colleague can point them at Item[1] 6 of Scott Meyers' "More Effective C++".

# 5.2   Searching for Bugs

So how does a code reviewer go about the business of hunting bugs in the code?

## 5.2.1   Local Analysis

At the core of all code reviews is a straightforward read of the code—file by file, function by function, line by line. For new code this typically means everything that's going to get checked in; for changes to existing code, this may just involve examination of the changed code.

The list of small gotchas to watch out for during this process depends enormously on the programming language in use, and to some extent on the type of software being developed. A starter list might include:

---

1   Which explains that prefix increment on user-defined types is more efficient that postfix increment because the latter has to create and destroy a temporary variable.

- Fencepost (or off-by-one) errors.
- Buffer overruns for fixed-size data structures (C's string handling library functions are notorious for this).
- Failure to code with exceptional returns from system calls (which may include `malloc` returning `NULL` or `new` throwing).
- Common typos (such as = rather than == in C-derived languages).

## 5.2.2  Data Structures

A useful viewpoint that can help to find trouble in code, particularly new code, is to consider the layout and structure of the data that the code manipulates. This data can take many forms—database tables, C structures, XML files—but similar considerations apply regardless.
- Check whether there are any issues with the lifetime of the data:
  - When are instances of data created, modified and destroyed?
  - Are creation and destruction operations appropriately symmetric?
  - Are there edge cases where resources can leak? This is particularly problematic when collections of interrelated data structures are created together (think transactions) or when asynchronous operations are used (what if the async operation never completes?).
- Check interactions between different data structures and between different areas of code that manipulate the same data structure:
  - Is the ownership of the data structure coherent between different components? If the same instance of a data structure is used by multiple chunks of code, are there edge cases where component A keeps using the instance even after component B has destroyed it? (Reference counted data structures can help with this.)
  - If the data structure is accessed simultaneously by different areas of code (under multithreading), is the access appropriately synchronized (mutexes, synchronized methods etc.)? If multiple locks are held, are they always acquired in a consistent order?
  - If the data structure is a keyed collection, is it guaranteed that the key will be unique?
- Check for internal consistency:
  - For fixed size containers, does the code respect the size restrictions?
  - Are pointers and references to other data structures guaranteed

to stay valid?

## 5.2.3  Scenario Walkthroughs

Another method for ensuring that new code does what it's supposed to is to dry-run mentally through some key scenarios for the code, and check that all of the required outputs from the code would be achieved.

- Ideally there will be use cases (see section 2.2, "Use Cases") for the code that illustrate the main-line paths that the code will take—these are ideal for scenario walkthroughs.
- Central loops on the most common execution sequences (the "golden path") can be examined for performance issues.
- Important error cases can also be examined where they diverge from the main-line paths through the code, to ensure that all code and data structures are tidied up correctly.
- On a smaller scale, if there are tricky bits of array manipulation or recursive code, working through a couple of test cases with a pencil and paper is often worthwhile.

# 5.3  Maintainability

## 5.3.1  Modularity

A key aspect of maintainability is appropriate modularity of the code. Good modularity reflects good design; each chunk of code is divided up so that its roles and responsibilities are clear—so when the code needs to be modified in future, there is an obvious place to make the change.

This is an excellent area for a code review to make a big difference. The programmer will have worked for days or weeks, evolving the code into its final form. Along the way, there's a good chance the overall structure of the code will have suffered. The code reviewer sees the code as a whole, and can look for poor choices of division.

The kinds of things that the reviewer can look out for are:
- When reading the code, do you have to jump backwards and forwards between lots of different files? If so, this may mean that related pieces of function are not being kept together.
- On a smaller scale, to follow a particular block of code, do you have to keep paging up to keep track of the enclosing control block (if, while etc.)? Code like this may well benefit from being encap-

sulated into a separate function (even if that function is only ever called from a single place).

- Are there any chunks of code that feel familiar because they're been copied and pasted from elsewhere? It's almost always better to have a single common function (which may need to be a little more generic); the chances of a future fix being applied to *both* copies of the code is small.

## 5.3.2 Communication

Much of the discussion in the rationale (see section 5.1, "Rationale: Why do code reviews?") behind code reviews revolved around *communication*: the code itself forms a means of communication between the person who understands the code now, and those who have to understand the code in future.

For some reason, programmers rarely have any difficulty believing that everyone else in the world is an idiot. This can be helpful for motivating good communication: "I want you to make your code so clear that not even a muppet could mess it up".

- Many of the apparently trivial things that tend to turn up in coding standards are about making this communication just that little bit more efficient: Longer, more descriptive names for identifiers make comprehension[2] of the code easier (provided they are well-chosen). They take longer to type, but successful code gets read many more times than it gets written.
- Consistent naming conventions across a chunk of software make typos much less likely. In the best-case scenario, this could save a fix-compile cycle; the worst-case scenario is, well, worse.
- Consistent indentation and layout makes reading the code slightly faster.

More significantly, there are a number of things that the code reviewer can look out for which may indicate that the code is not as clear as it could be.

- Are there enough comments to enable the code to be read and understood in a single pass? If the code needs to be re-read several times before it comes clear, more comments or a restructuring of the code may help.

---

2   It's possible to take this to extremes, however. I once reviewed some code that was equivalent to `for (ii=0; ii<len; len++)`, but when I mentioned the infinite loop to the programmer he couldn't see it—the variable names he'd used in place of `ii` and `len` were so long that the key typo was off the side of his editor screen!

- Is there any code that the reviewer initially thinks is wrong, but eventually realizes is actually correct? If so, other readers of the code are likely to reach the same incorrect conclusion, so a comment explaining the likely misconception will help.
- Do the names of functions and variables accurately reflect their purpose? A function called ClearScreen would be expected to clear the screen or return an error—any other behaviour would be perverse and confusing. Ten or fifteen minutes spent coming up with exactly the right name for a function is time well spent, if it prevents future confusion.
- Are related areas of function obviously related according to their names? For example, ABCAllocateXYZ and ABCFreeXYZ are an obvious pair that would be expected to have symmetric effects.
- Is the same terminology used consistently throughout the code? This can be particularly important to help people who are not native English speakers—using four different synonyms for the same thing is likely to confuse. The most common or standard terminology for a particular concept is usually the best choice.
- Are there pointless comments cluttering up the code? This often occurs in environments where metrics covering the ratio of comment lines to code lines are tracked (see subsection 9.1.1, "Metrics"), and results in comments like:
```
// Increment loop variable
++ii;
```

The key theme to point out here is the Principle of Least Astonishment: what's the most obvious guess for what the code does, and is this what it *actually* does?

# 5.4 The Code Review Process

## 5.4.1 Logistics

The logistics of the code review process are fairly straightforward, but there are a number of small points that help to keep the process as efficient as possible. The net result of the process should be that both the coder and the reviewer are happy for the final version of the code to be checked in and used.

- The coder prepares the code for review. This should make life as easy as possible for the reviewer (if only to keep them in a good mood!).

- Put the code into an accessible, standard place.
- For changed code, provide a copy of the unmodified "before" code for comparison purposes.
- For a second or later iteration of the code review process, also provide the previously submitted versions of the code so that the reviewer can confirm that problems that they've pointed out before have been correctly fixed.
- Once the code has been provided for review, don't change it without checking with the reviewer.
- Make sure the code passes any mechanical checks that are required—for example, that it clean compiles, or that its layout complies with any coding standards
- If there is supplementary information, such as a bug report, a design document or a specification, make sure this is available for the reviewer.
- If a preliminary version of the code is being reviewed, indicate which parts are likely to change and which are considered complete.
- Perform a quick sanity-check dry run of the code review, to confirm that all the code is in place and has the correct version.
- If previous code reviews have raised the same problem several times, ensure that nothing analogous exists in the current code.
- The reviewer generates feedback comments on the code.
  - Make it clear what needs to be done about each comment, whether it's answering a question, adding a comment or fixing the code itself—or even nothing at all.
  - Use a consistent method for correlating the comments with the code. This may involve changing the code itself using a specific marker, or providing file and line number information.
  - If a particular problem applies in many places in the code, make it clear that all of them need to be changed (the word *passim* can be used to indicate this).
  - If necessary, categorize the comments according to the expected code changes. One possible classification is to describe the type of change (e.g. W=wrong code, O=omitted, S=superfluous, P=performance, M=maintainability) and the severity (e.g. 1=would cause crash, 2=major loss of function, 3=minor loss of function, 4=cosmetic).
- The coder deals with the code review comments. For many of the comments, this just involves answering the relevant question or

making the required markups. However, there are often code review comments that the coder disagrees with—after all, the coder is still the person who knows the code the best and who is ultimately responsible for the code. For these comments, the coder has to convince the reviewer of their point of view. (A common situation in these cases is for the reviewer to respond: "Ah, I understand now. Please add that explanation as a comment in the code").

- Repeat as necessary: with less experienced programmers, it's often necessary to repeat the above steps until both the programmer and the reviewer are happy that the code can be checked in. If this is the case, the reviewer needs to make clear to the programmer which parts of the code need to be re-reviewed.
- If there are any items of contention that the coder and the reviewer can't reach agreement on, escalate them to the team leader.
- Track as necessary: depending on the management environment, it may be required or useful to keep track of a number of things during the code review process (see subsection 9.1.1, "Metrics").
  - Pre- and post- review versions of the code may need to be kept.
  - Code review comments may need to be kept for future reference.
  - Classification of code review markups by severity and type may be worth tracking, to help indicate components that appear particular difficult (and so may need more extensive testing) or to monitor the performance of the programmer.
  - Time taken in both the review and the markup process may need to be tracked against a project plan.

## 5.4.2  Dialogue

Software developers can be extremely protective of their code, which means that some of them end up treating code reviews as a personal attack on their competence. It's important to defuse these kind of tensions as much as possible; one way to do this is to deal with the code review process as a dialogue.

The reviewer has the most important role in keeping this dialogue civilized.

- Remain polite at all times.
- Use questions rather than assertions. "Will this chunk of code cope

with ..." is better than "Simply Wrong[3]".

- Make it clear comments are subjective as often as possible. "I found SomeFn() hard to follow because ..." is better than "SomeFn() is incomprehensible".
- Clearly distinguish between stylistic and semantic markups; there's a big difference between "this is wrong" and "this isn't how I'd have coded this". Some school teachers mark in a red pen and a green pen—the red for errors that would lose marks, the green for improvements in clarity or structure.
- Try to imagine and provide theoretical future changes to the code that back up any maintainability concerns: "I'm worried that in future someone might assume that SomeFn() doesn't lock and use it from within a locked section ...".
- Don't forget to comment on the positive as well as the negative: "I really liked the hashtable code—I'll have to borrow that technique for other code."

That said, the coder also has to bear a number of things in mind.

- Also remain polite at all times.
- Remember that you're not capable of judging whether your code is difficult for someone else to understand—you can almost never refuse to add more explanatory comments.
- If a reviewer requests a change in an chunk of code, and you know that the same comment applies to another similar chunk of code, then volunteer to change that too.

## 5.5  Common Mistakes

The most common mistake that turns up in the code review process is that the reviewer doesn't review the code thoroughly enough. This is particularly common when code reviews have been mandated by management fiat, without any training on the process of code reviewing and without allowing enough time and resources to do the job properly.

This kind of shallow, "syntax-only" review can occasionally find small bugs, but more often it's a waste of time that only turns up trivial things (like breaches of coding standards) that should be being caught automatically by the build process anyway (see subsection 4.6.3, "Enforcing Standards").

So for a reviewer, the most important question is: did you understand

---

3    A friend of mine once acquired a rubber stamp with the words "SIMPLY WRONG" in red capitals; while amusing, this is hardly likely to engender the right spirit.

the code?

If not, then the whole code review process is a waste. None of the reasons for doing a code review in the first place (see section 5.1, "Rationale: Why do code reviews?") are fulfilled:

- The reviewer can't judge the correctness of the code and spot the deep, nasty bugs if they don't understand the code.
- The code either isn't maintainable (and that's why the reviewer didn't understand it) or the reviewer hasn't taken the time to tell whether it's maintainable or not.
- The reviewer hasn't been educated about the form and function of the code, so that knowledge is still locked in the coder's head.

A useful self-check for a reviewer is to consider an obscure test case (perhaps a timing window, or a resource acquisition failure): will the code cope with it or not? If you can't tell, then the review probably hasn't been thorough enough (if you can tell, and it won't, then obviously that will be one of the review comments!).

If the reviewer didn't understand the code because it was too difficult to understand—the comments were nonexistent, the documentation was missing, and the code itself was confusing—then there's a problem with the maintainability of the code. To get decent quality software, that problem needs to be fixed.

If the reviewer didn't understand the code because they've not taken the time to do it properly, then there are a couple of possibilities. Firstly, they may just need more practice in code reviewing—hopefully the advice in this chapter and in the section on ramping up on a new codebase should help with that (see section 7.2, "Learning a Codebase").

More likely, though, is that a policy of code reviewing has been imposed without allowing sufficient time for the reviewer to actually make a difference. A thorough code review for a new chunk of code can take 10% of the time it took to write the code, or even as high as 20% if the reviewer is completely new to the area. This is time worth investing, as it increases the quality of the code and doubles the number of people who understand it thoroughly.

# 6 TEST

Once a piece of software has been built, it needs to be tested to check that it does actually do what it's supposed to do. This has always been an area that six-nines development takes very seriously; the testing phase is the proving ground to determine how close the software is to that magical 99.9999% number. More recently, this heavy emphasis on testing has started to become common in other development sectors—in particular, the Test Driven Development aspect of Extreme Programming.

This chapter is also going to cover a slightly wider area than purely testing itself, as the testing process involves a number of sub-steps:

- The test itself: run the code in some configuration, and look for incorrect behaviour.
- Find problems and narrow down the circumstances involved (in other words, generate a *reproduction scenario*).
- Debug the problems.
- Fix the problems.
- Re-test to confirm that the problem has been solved.

## 6.1 How

Testing checks that the software does what it's supposed to do. This immediately illustrates a direct connection between the requirements for the software (see chapter 2, "Requirements") and (some of) the testing phase: the requirements say what the software should do, and the testing shows what it does do. Both of these concern the customer's view of the system: what where they expecting, what did they get, and do they match?

However, not all testing is done from the point of view of the user (whether that user is an actual human user, or another software component of a larger system). In this chapter we're going to roughly distinguish between two main styles of testing:

- *Black box testing*: testing a system purely by using its external interfaces, effectively with no knowledge of the internal details of the implementation (see section 3.1, "Interfaces and Implementations")
- *White box testing*: testing a system with full knowledge of the details of its implementation (sometimes known as crystal box testing, which actually makes more logical sense).

There are also many different phases of testing.

- *Unit testing*: building test harnesses to check that particular components of the software fulfil their interfaces.
- *Coverage testing*: generating particular tests aimed at the difficult-to-reach nooks and crannies in the code, with the aim of hitting them in the lab before they get hit in the field.
- *Integration testing*: testing multiple components integrated together.
- *Functional verification (FV) testing*: testing the system as a whole to confirm that the functional requirements are satisfied—in other words, confirming that it does what it says on the tin.
- *System testing*: testing the whole system in more stressful environments that are at least as bad as the real world (large numbers of users, network delays, hardware failures, etc.).
- *Interoperability testing*: confirming that the software works well with other software that's supposed to do the same thing[1].
- *Performance testing*: scaling the system up to large numbers (of users, connections, links or whatever) to confirm that performance holds up. This can involve a considerable amount of investment, in extra hardware or scalability test harnesses or both.
- *Free-form testing*: randomly trying to drive the system in weird and wacky ways. Particularly relevant for systems with a user interface.
- *Install testing*: checking that any installer packages correctly detect and cope with a variety of different destination environments (see subsection 4.6.5, "Delivering the Code").

Not all types of software need all of these phases, but higher quality software is likely to use almost all of them.

---

1   Even if that other software is doing things that are technically incorrect. Customers don't actually care if a Cisco router has some detail of a routing protocol wrong—they expect it to just work.

# 6.2  Who and When

There is occasionally debate within the software industry as to whether it's better to have a separate test team, or to have the development team perform the majority of the testing. Each approach has its own advantages.

A separate test team allows development and testing to proceed in parallel, and can involve specialists in testing mechanisms (for example, properly testing new versions of a consumer operating system like Microsoft Windows or Linux involves a vast array of different hardware and software combinations). Dedicated testers are inherently black box testers; they only test based on the interface to the code, because they have no idea what the implementation of the code is.

Testing within the development team means that the people with the best knowledge of the code are doing the testing; they know which areas are likely to be fragile, and where the performance bottlenecks are likely to be—in other words, they are able to do white box testing. This kind of testing can also often be automated—regularly repeating tests as part of the overnight build system (see subsection 4.6.4, "Building the Code") is good way to improve confidence in the quality level of the code.

In the end, the choice between these two approaches comes down to a balance driven by the particular scenario, and a mixture of both styles of testing is often the best course for a large project.

However, if testing is done within the development team, it's usually worth having someone other than the developer of a component do some testing on that component. This has a couple of advantages: firstly, knowledge about that component gets more widely spread within the team; secondly, a different pair of eyes will have different implicit assumptions and so will come at the tests in a way that may expose incorrect assumptions that went into the code.

As well as debate as to *who* should test software, there is also some debate in the software industry as to *when* software should be tested. Writing the tests before the code itself is one of the central tenets of Extreme Programming (XP). As with iterative development cycles (see section 2.1, "Waterfall versus Agile"), this arise from taking a principle of good software engineering practice to its extreme: testing is a Good Thing, so push it to the forefront of the development activity.

Obviously, test-first is much more suited to black box style tests than white box style testing; it's also difficult to produce good integration tests in advance of the code being written. However, test-first also involves an important factor which can be both an advantage and a disadvantage:

| Test Type | Black/White Box | Automatable |
|---|---|---|
| Unit | White | Yes |
| Coverage | White | Mostly |
| Integration | White | Yes |
| Functional Verification | Black | Yes |
| System | Black | No |
| Interoperability | Black | Not usually |
| Performance | Black | Sometimes |
| Free-form | Black | No |

**Table 6.1: Styles and automation possibilities for different types of test**

it's much more difficult to reduce the amount of testing in the face of an impending deadline when the effort has already been spent.

In real world software projects, deferring some functionality or some testing beyond a fixed release date (with the expectation of higher support loads and a follow-on release later) can be an unavoidable response to a difficult situation. Any such potential gains in the schedule are heavily reduced if the corresponding test code has already been written.

Pragmatically, though, the mere fact that proper testing is getting done is much more important than the details of the phasing of that testing.

# 6.3  Psychology of Testing

*I believe that the final bug in TEX was discovered and removed on November 27, 1985. But if, somehow, an error still lurks in the code, I shall gladly pay a finder's fee of $20.48 to the first person who discovers it. (This is twice the previous amount, and I plan to double it again in a year; you see, I really am confident!)*[2]

For some reason, the vast majority of new programmers come equipped with an excessive over-confidence about their own code. They're absolutely convinced that they've written great code that doesn't have any bugs in it. Even after the first few bugs are demonstrated to them, they will then believe that those are the only bugs and the rest of the code is perfect.

This hubris even affects those who should know better. When Donald Knuth—one of the world's most highly respected computer scientists—

---

2　Donald E. Knuth, Preface to "TEX: The Program".

released his T$_E$X typesetting system he was convinced it was bug-free and offered a bug bounty that would double each year. In the end, the bounty was capped; there have been almost a hundred changes to the code since that pronouncement.

One of the key things that differentiates an experienced software engineer from a junior programmer is a visceral understanding that with code comes bugs. Once this is understood, the testing process starts to change from being a boring drag to being a vital safety net between you and the consequences of your bugs. Part of high-quality software engineering is to fully accept this concept, and plan for it accordingly—with extensive testing and also with code reviews, support structures, built-in diagnostics and so on.

This also gives a special emphasis to coverage testing. All code has bugs, and the only chance we have of reducing those bugs is by testing and fixing the code; to a first approximation it's simplest to assume that code that's not been tested is broken. So, if 10% of the code has never been hit during all of the test phases, then that particular 10% is effectively broken—and this will show up when it does get hit, out in the field.

Of course, understanding how important testing is doesn't alter the fact that it can be very dull. The other factor that can help to motivate programmers towards testing is to make the testing as programmatic as possible. Programmers generally enjoy writing code; if much of their testing involves writing test harness code, then this will be more enjoyable than, say, manually driving a GUI through a pre-determined sequence of test steps. Programmatic test code also helps to make it easy to repeat tests with minimal effort later (see section 6.4, "Regressibility"). However, remember that test code is still code—and so still contains bugs itself. It's often worth deliberately and temporarily inserting a bug into the product code to confirm that the test code will indeed raise an alarm appropriately.

In addition to an acknowledgement of fallibility, good testing also involves a particular mindset: vicious and bloody-minded. A good tester is actively looking for things to fail, and trying as hard as possible to generate that failure. Experience of the kinds of bugs that show up in software gives a good toolbox of nasty things to try.

- Range checks: If the code expects to receive values between 1 and 100, does it cope with 0, 1, 99, 100, 101? Does it cope with 1,000,000? The specification for your system may not have included a need for it to scale that high, but it's good to know *in advance* what would happen if someone tries—does it fail gracefully or catastrophically?
- Unchecked input: If the code is expecting an integer, what happens

if it gets a string or a floating point number? If a text field is a fixed size, what happens if too much text is entered? What happens if the user enters 29th February into a date field? On a non-leap year? What happens on a web system if HTML is included in an entry field that expects plain text? What happens if a malformed packet arrives? What happens if the length fields for the components of a serialized data structure don't add up?

- Timing windows: What happens when lots of different things happen at once? What if the user deletes the file at the same time as getting the application to perform a time-consuming operation on it?
- Scalability: What happens when just lots of things happen? What happens when the disk is full? What happens when a file gets too big for the filesystem? What happens if you have $2^{12}$, $2^{24}$ or $2^{32}$ pieces of data?

With all of this cunning testing, it's easy to forget the essentials: testing the system in the kinds of scenarios that will happen in the real world. For networking software, this involves testing that the code interoperates with standard networking equipment, such as Cisco and Juniper routers. For web-based software, this means checking that all of the web pages work with the browsers that people use—Internet Explorer, Firefox, Safari—in the configurations they use them (e.g. 1024x768 for laptop users). For systems that have a user interface, it involves checking that common actions are easy to perform and that there are no glitches which would infuriate heavy users. Use cases from the original requirements process can be very helpful for this kind of testing (see section 2.2, "Use Cases").

# 6.4  Regressibility

Once a test has been done, how easy is it to repeat the test? If the test succeeded at some point, is it easy to confirm that later versions of the code still pass the test? If the test case failed and a bug had to be fixed, can we check that the bug hasn't reappeared?

These questions give us the phrase *regression testing*—confirming that later code incarnations have not regressed the correct behaviour of earlier code versions. To make answering these questions feasible and efficient, the testing framework for the code should be *regressible*.

The key motivation behind this desire for regressibility is that bugs should only ever need to be fixed *once*, because fixing bugs takes valuable time that could have been spent writing more code. A large part of only fixing bugs once resolves down to good coding and design practices: if there is only a single component with a particular responsibility, and no code is ever copied and pasted, then it's unlikely that the same bug will occur in multiple places in the code.

The rest of what's needed to make it unlikely that bugs will ever be fixed more than once boils down to the overall framework for software development, especially the testing framework:

- Software identification & versioning: It must be possible to exactly identify which versions of the code are implicated in a particular test case (whether successful or failed)—which means that reliable code control, build and versioning systems are needed (see subsection 4.6.1, "Revision Control").
- Bug tracking: Developers and testers need to be able to report and track bugs in the software in a way that makes it easy to spot duplicate bug reports, and to correlate bug reports with the code versions (see subsection 4.6.2, "Other Tracking Systems").
- Test case tracking: Likewise, testers need to be able to track which test cases correlate to which potential bugs, on what dates.
- Automation: Whenever possible, test cases should only need human interaction when they are initially written and first run; after that, it should be possible to automatically run the test case and programmatically check for success or failure without human intervention.

A large battery of automatically-run, thorough tests that can be run at the click of a button allows a huge boost to the confidence levels about the safety of a new piece of code (particularly for properly paranoid developers, see section 6.3, "Psychology of Testing").

Of course, this isn't always possible. GUIs in particular are often difficult to test in a regressible manner, even with input-replay tools designed for this situation. However, as described in the next section, using a design (such as the Model/View/Controller (MVC) design pattern) that makes the UI as trivial and separable as possible will alleviate this problem.

## 6.5  Design for Testability

The previous section argued that to get high-quality, reliably-tested software, the whole development system needs to allow automated, thorough testing of the code.

However, this isn't something that can be bolted on after the fact; the code and the development framework need to be designed from the ground up to allow for the regressible test framework.

A trivial example should help to make this clear. Imagine a software system that needs to run on a machine with limited memory—it might be a super-huge database system that exhausts the virtual memory of a mainframe, or it could be a game for a mobile phone with a small fixed amount of flash RAM. This software needs to be able to cope with the memory running out; in C terms, all calls to malloc need to cope with a null pointer being returned.

How do you test whether all of this code really does cope with null? One possibility is to set up a test machine with limited amounts of memory, and try to tune things so that all of the possible malloc calls get hit. However, this probably isn't going to be a test that's easy to repeat, which augurs long nights debugging memory allocation problems in the future.

Instead, if the code were originally designed and written to call a wrapper function rather than malloc[3], then it would be easy to replace that wrapper with code that generates allocation failures on demand. That way, a test case could (say) set things up so that the fourth call to the malloc wrapper fails, and thus hit whatever arms of code are needed without any of that tedious mucking about with exhausting real memory.

This is a fairly straightforward example, which is a particular instance of a wider approach to aid testability: wrap all system calls, so that fake ones can be substituted when necessary for testing.

The idea of wrapping system calls is itself a particular instance of a wider strategy for allowing the thorough, regressible testing that's needed for top-quality software systems: eliminate all sources of non-determinism in the system. Another facet of this strategy is to tightly control multi-threaded code (see section 4.3, "Multithreading"), so that all inter-thread interactions can be intercepted and simulated for testing, if necessary. Similarly, wrapping any timer-related code allows deterministic testing of timing window cases.

The Model-View-Controller architectural design pattern described elsewhere (see subsection 3.2.1, "Component Responsibility") also illustrates this principle: the individual parts of the pattern can each be tested in a predictable way.

To implement this strategy of controlling non-determinism in the system, it has to be planned for and designed for from the beginning. The level of software quality required should be decided at the start of the project (see section 2.3, "Implicit Requirements"), and the only way to reach the higher levels of quality is to plan for the testing framework at the design

---

3   In C++, the equivalent can be done in a straightforward way by overriding operator new.

stage.

Another example: planning for coverage testing (that is, tracking exactly which lines of code are hit during the test cases). Code coverage numbers are easily generated on desktop systems and above, but generating them on embedded systems may involve building in statistics by hand.

It is worth pointing out that this correlation between quality level and testing frameworks goes both ways: there are plenty of types and styles of software where a fully-regressible, wrapped-system-call, automated test system is overkill. To return to the `malloc` example, for many "normal" applications running on a desktop system, code that checks for a failed allocation (and tests that exercise that code) are probably overkill—if the virtual memory system of modern operating systems fails to allocate 100 bytes, then the machine is probably on its way down anyway[4].

## 6.6 Debugging

Debugging goes hand in hand with testing: once a test case uncovers a bug, that bug will (usually) need to be fixed. Debugging always extends beyond any formal test phase; no matter how conscientious and comprehensive the testing, the real world always turns up things that weren't covered. To put it another way, a horde of real users (or an interoperability test with a real device) is whole new testing experience: it's hard to make anything idiot-proof, as idiots are so very ingenious.

The most important thing to understand about debugging are the factors that make debugging easier: diagnostics and determinism.

Diagnostics are vitally important to be sure that a problem has really occurred, and to understand the steps that led up to the problem. In an ideal world, a suitable collection of diagnostic facilities will be built into the system for this (see subsection 3.2.4, "Diagnostics"). In a less ideal world, one of the steps involved in tracking down a tricky problem will often be the addition of more diagnostics.

Determinism is even more important for debugging than for testing (see section 6.5, "Design for Testability"), because the reliable link between cause and effect allows the investigation to proceed in logical steps. In testing, determinism ensures that the output of a test is known, and so can be checked that it is correct. In debugging, determinism allows the failure case to be repeated, as the investigation narrows in on the source of the

---

4 One unashamedly pragmatic approach to a failed `malloc` call is for the program to just `sleep` for a while; that way, the first program with a core dump in the system error logs will be someone else's.

problem.

Without these two key pillars of debugging, finding the root cause of a problem is much more difficult. For example, debugging multithreading problems is notoriously difficult (see section 4.3, "Multithreading") because the determinism requirement fails so badly.

# 7 SUPPORT

The support phase of a software project happens when the code is out there working in the real world, rather than in the development environment. In the real world it's exposed to an unpredictable new factor: users. These users will complain of problems in the software, both real and imagined; the support organization for the software has to deal with these complaints.

Depending on the type of the software and the type of customer, the support organization may well be split into a number of levels. For example:

- Level 1 support might deal with answering the support phone line and confirming that the problem is in the supported software.
- Level 2 support might install missing product upgrades and patches, and might spot duplicates of already-known problems.
- Level 3 support might guide a user through the process of running test scenarios and gathering diagnostic information.
- Level 4 support might be the support engineers who actually have access to the source code and are able to make fixes and generate patches.

In this chapter, we're concentrating on the highest level of support: when a (potentially) genuine bug reaches a team that has the capability of fixing that bug. This situation is a little bit different from software development—and it's an area that is oddly absent from software engineering literature[1].

---

1  Perhaps again reflecting most software engineers' deeply-held belief that their code has no bugs.

## 7.1  Customers

Somewhere on the trail between the users and the software developers are the *customers*—the people who are paying for the software and as a result expect it to work.

Entire books have been written about customer management, but there are some core essentials that can make the difference between a happy customer and a customer who's reaching for the nearest lawyer.

The main idea is to build a relationship with the customer, so that they feel that they can trust the support organization. Having a consistent point of contact helps with this, as does providing regular updates on the status of any outstanding support requests.

The best way of getting a customer to feel that they can trust the support team is if they actually can trust the support team—in other words, if the support team never lies to the customer, no matter how tempting it might be. In the long term, the truth is easier to keep track of and there's no chance of being caught out. Expressing things as probabilities rather than certainties can help with this: "I'm 80% sure we've found the problem" is often more accurate than "We've fixed that already, it's on its way".

It's also worth being as up-front as possible about bad news. If a problem can't be fixed, or if the timescales are going to be much worse that the customer needs, it's better to tell them sooner rather than later—if nothing else, it gives the support team a longer period in which to calm the customer down.

Finally, for many software development sectors it's worth bearing in mind the problem of requirements (see chapter 2, "Requirements"). The customer often knows the problem domain much better than the software team does, and so querying the customer for more information on what they're really trying to do can often illuminate frustrating problems.

## 7.2  Learning a Codebase

Support engineers often find that they need to learn about an unfamiliar codebase in a hurry. Ideally, the first place to look for general information about the software is the documentation (see subsection 3.4.3, "Documentation"). However, in practice it's often necessary to work things out from the source code alone.

The first technique for ramping up on a new codebase from its source code is to follow the flow of the code. Starting from `main`, and with the assistance of a source code navigation tool, build a picture of the call hierarchy of the program. It's helpful to write this hierarchy down on paper—that way you're forced to actually look at the code in detail, so you're more likely to remember it, and more likely to spot unusual things that bear further examination.

The next technique that helps to understand an unfamiliar codebase is to follow the flow of the data. Start with global variables, which typically hold the roots of any collections of data (and which are easy to spot, with nm if nothing else). Follow this with a search for any dynamically created data structures (by searching for new or malloc), to determine how they are organized and what their lifetimes are. It's usually worth sketching a diagram of the main data structures and how they inter-relate as you go, whether in UML or some less formal notation. Again, doing this by hand rather than by using an automated system forces you to actually look at the code, and to make judgements about which data structures are essential and which are merely auxiliaries.

Finally, it's always helpful to work through the flow of the code and the data for the key scenarios that the code supports (see section 2.2, "Use Cases"). This can be done in a debugger, by examining comprehensive trace output (see section 4.5, "Tracing"), or just by stepping through the code in an editor.

## 7.3  Imperfect Code

Although this book as a whole is aimed at the business of producing high quality code, the support phase for a product sometimes involves dealing with the consequences of low quality code. In this situation, pragmatic compromises are often necessary—an ideal solution to a slew of bugs might be to re-write a particular component, but that's not always possible under pressure of deadlines and resources.

So how to make the best of a bad situation?

The first recommendation for improving the quality of the codebase over the longer term is to improve the testability of the code. It's easy to get into a situation where every new fix to the codebase induces a new bug somewhere else, like trying to press air bubbles out from under linoleum. This is particularly bad because it generates a position where copy and paste becomes the pragmatically correct thing to do: if scenario A shows up a bug in code X, but code X is also used for scenarios B, C, D, E ... that can't be tested, then the safest thing to do is to clone X so that just scenario A uses the copied, fixed code X'. The best cure for this is to build a suite of regression tests that can catch these potentially-induced problems; this makes it much safer for support engineers that don't know the codebase very well to make fixes.

Adding new test cases and extending the test framework will automatically result in the next recommendation, which is to make fixes slowly and thoroughly. For poorer quality code, it's commensurately more important to run related test scenarios, to add or update comments, to hunt for similar code that might need the same fix, to update what documentation exists and so on.

In particular, refactoring related code as part of a bug fix helps to improve the codebase for the next time around—for example, merging copied and pasted code into a single common function can often be done safely and reliably.

These may not sound like vast improvements, but over time they can make a substantial difference. One (not six-nines!) codebase I worked on had a reputation as a support black hole, needing one or two support engineers on it full time; nine months later, this was down to one or two days a week from a single engineer (an 80% reduction in the support load). The difference was that the new, more skilled, support team were more careful and took longer over each fix, and so rarely introduced new bugs.

# 7.4  Support Metrics

A key premise of this book is that investing in higher-quality software is worth the up-front investment in the long term. The support phase of a project supports[2] this assertion by providing the statistical data to back it up.

Generating these statistics needs raw data; the first place this comes from is the bug tracking system. A bug tracking system makes sure that no bugs get lost; there's either a fix or an explicit decision not to fix the bug. Consistently including a little more tracking information (some of which can be tracked mechanically) into the system provides a wealth of additional statistical data:

- Bug severity: How severe is the problem? This might range from an entire system crash with lost and corrupted data, to a typographical error in some displayed text.
- Bug urgency: How important is the bug? This may not be correlated with severity—a glaring typo on the welcome screen might be more urgent to fix than a system crash that only happens in extremely

---

2   Pun unintentional.

obscure and unlikely situations.

- Time invested: How much time is involved in generating the fix? This could be the calendar time elapsed between reporting and fixing the bug, or (more usefully) the amount of developer resource invested in fixing the bug.
- Extent of code change: How many lines of code were changed as part of the fix, and by whom?
- Cause of bug: Was the bug induced by an earlier change, or has it lurked undetected for a while?

All of this data reveals any number of interesting things about the codebase (assuming enough data has been accumulated to make the statistics sound):

- Which components and modules have had the highest number of bugs, per line of code? This may indicate components that are worth reviewing, refactoring or even rewriting.
- Which areas of code have had the largest amount developer effort invested in fixes for them? Again, this may indicate poor components—or just poorly documented components.
- Which developers have fixed the most bugs? And what proportion of those fixes have induced more bugs later? This may indicate which members of the support team need to slow down and be more thorough.
- Which bugs were the most difficult to fix? This might be indicated by bugs that had a lot of time and resource invested in them, but which only resulted in a small code change. This may indicate a flaw in the underlying design that needs to be re-examined, or maybe that the testing and diagnostics features of the code are insufficient.

These can all help direct refactoring and support efforts to where they'll be most effective. However, as ever when metrics are measured, remember that people will adjust their behaviour to optimize the metric rather than the (more nebulous) actual quality.

It's surprisingly rare for there to be up-front estimates of the cost of support for software projects. When there are such estimates, they're usually too low—because the estimates are made by the development engineers who

- have little or no experience in support
- believe their own code to be bug-free anyway (see section 6.3, "Psychology of Testing").

With comprehensive measurements of the support costs of previous projects in place, it's much easier to make these estimates more accurate.

By correlating across different styles of development for the original development projects, it's also data that will convince higher levels of management of the long term benefits of higher quality software development processes.

# 8  Planning a Project

High quality software involves more than just writing better code, or even than just ensuring that the code is tested rigorously. Reliability is not an accident; it is designed for and planned for.

This chapter discusses that process of planning a high-quality software project. As with other places in this book, the general principles are shared with other forms of software development, but high-quality development needs to be more predictable. Planning has to be more accurate since there's much less scope for dropping features as the ship date looms. The compensating factors that make it possible to plan more accurately are that

- the specification is more likely to be fixed and coherent (see section 2.1, "Waterfall versus Agile") than for other development sectors
- the development is more likely to use tried and proven technology (see subsection 3.2.5, "Avoiding the Cutting Edge").

## 8.1  Estimation

Early on in the career of a software engineer, they are almost certain to get asked to estimate how long a particular piece of code will take.

By default, programmers are inherently dreadful at coming up with estimates. I've never encountered a new programmer who was naturally able to come up with accurate estimates, no matter how skilled they were in the actual business of writing code—and their estimates are always too low, never too high.

As they get more experienced, programmers do slowly become more accurate in their estimates, but often in a very ad-hoc way: they take their original estimates and just double (or in some cases triple) them. As the project progresses, if they end up with too much time, they can then find some interesting extra things to code in order to fill up the time.

It's not just the lower echelons of the software world that have problems with estimation; IT projects in general are legendary for their overruns (in both calendar time and resource time) and their failures to deliver. Getting the plan seriously wrong is anathema for a high-quality software development—the first thing to get dropped is always the quality bar for the code.

So what's the best way to tackle the problems of estimation?

## 8.1.1  Task Estimation

The first stage is to improve the accuracy of developers' estimates of individual tasks, and experience is the best way to do this. From an early stage, it's important that even junior developers should be coming up with sizings for their tasks, and should then be comparing the reality with the estimate once the dust has settled.

Learning quickly involves getting as much information as possible out of the data. To get the most out of experiences with estimation, developers need to preserve their original estimates, track their progress against them as the task progresses, and perform a retrospective analysis after the task is done. The last is key: looking back at why and how the estimates were missed helps with both a quantitative analysis of the process, and also helps to grind down the insane over-optimism that so many young developers have. Having a gung-ho, "can do" attitude is all very well, but when applied to estimation it causes disasters.

For a project manager, one particularly mean-but-educational trick is to get a junior developer to commit to a completion date for a task based on their own hugely optimistic estimates—while secretly expecting and planning that the task will take rather longer. Either the developer will be embarrassed because they miss their predictions massively, or they'll find themselves having to work ridiculously hard to hit them. In either case, it helps to bring home the problems of under-estimation in a visceral way—and they'll be more cautious the next time around.

For a developer to take an estimate seriously, they have to agree that the estimates are reasonable and sensible. Getting the developers to come up with their own estimates is one way to do this; another is to make sure they are able to give feedback when other people's estimates are imposed on them. This is particularly true when they think the imposed estimates are too low—to do otherwise puts the developer in a position where they can win an argument by doing *less* work.

Another thing to emphasize is that estimates are supposed to be wrong—that's why they're *estimates*. The only way to get a completely accurate estimate is to give the estimate after the task has been done, which is hardly useful. What's important, therefore, is that the margin of error isn't too large, and that there are errors in both directions: sometimes over-estimating, sometimes under-estimating, so that in the long run things balance out.

To reduce the margin of error, it's often worth coming at the estimate from several different directions, and comparing the results. Get two different people to estimate the same task, or estimate it in terms of lines of code, man-days, percentage size of a related chunk of existing code, etc. (see subsection 9.1.1, "Metrics").

On an over-estimated task, it's very easy for a developer to pad out the work so that their task comes in exactly on schedule. To avoid this, it's worth emphasizing this inherent imprecision of estimates—good estimates are expected to come in early sometimes as well as late sometimes. That way, if a developer has over-estimated one out of several tasks, they will bring that task in early so that it can balance out other tasks that are coming in late.

To put it another way, consider the distribution of the errors in a collection of estimates. An ideal situation is that these errors should form a bell curve around zero, with as narrow a distribution as possible. The more uncertainties there were in the original estimates—perhaps because the estimates were made before enough details were known, or because the project relies on some new technology (see subsection 3.2.5, "Avoiding the Cutting Edge")—the larger the standard deviation of their accuracy. If developers are constantly padding out their work on over-estimated tasks, and slipping under-estimated tasks, then the distribution will look very different from this symmetrical bell curve.

## 8.1.2  Project Estimation

Once developers are capable of making sensible estimates for individual tasks, the more daunting problem is how to put a collection of such estimates together to produce an overall project plan.

Building such a collection of estimates can't be done without a design. The design describes how the big problem is subdivided into smaller problems, and more detailed designs break those in turn into components, subcomponents, objects, tasks and subtasks. As the design becomes more detailed, so the accuracy level of the overall estimates becomes higher.

| | A | B | C | D |
|---|---|---|---|---|
| | Task | Original Estimate | | Notes |
| 1 | | | | |
| 2 | | Days | kLoC | |
| 3 | | | | |
| 4 | Design/Code/Unit Test | 203.5 | 24.1 | |
| 5 | Framework | 31.0 | 3.3 | |
| 6 | Initialization | 7.0 | 1.0 | Boilerplate code so expect higher productivity |
| 7 | OS interaction | 3.0 | 0.4 | |
| 8 | MIB registration | 7.0 | 0.8 | |
| 9 | Local interface determination | 8.0 | 0.3 | Non-portable; prototyping needed |
| 10 | Socket(s) setup | 6.0 | 0.8 | |
| 11 | Config/Management | 48.5 | 8.4 | |
| 12 | SNMP parsing | 4.0 | 0.5 | |
| 13 | MIB processing | 7.0 | 3.0 | Semi-autogenerated code |
| 14 | Data structure walking | 5.5 | 0.5 | |
| 15 | Command line processing | 12.0 | 2.0 | |
| 16 | Display code | 13.0 | 1.4 | |
| 17 | Logging framework | 7.0 | 1.0 | |
| 18 | Link State Processing | 55.0 | 5.5 | |
| 19 | LSDB management | 8.0 | 0.8 | |
| 20 | Flooding | 7.5 | 0.8 | |
| 21 | LSA processing | 17.0 | 1.7 | |
| 22 | Local interface processing | 2.0 | 0.4 | |
| 23 | Interface FSM | 6.0 | 0.3 | |
| 24 | Stub areas | 7.0 | 0.7 | |
| 25 | Not-so-stubby-areas | 4.0 | 0.4 | |
| 26 | External route processing | 3.5 | 0.4 | |
| 27 | Route Calculation | 33.0 | 3.4 | |
| 28 | SPF calculation | 11.0 | 0.8 | Subtle code so lower productivity expected |
| 29 | Area boundary processing | 7.5 | 1.0 | |
| 30 | AS boundary processing | 5.5 | 0.7 | |
| 31 | AS external route calculation | 5.0 | 0.5 | |
| 32 | Route table publish | 4.0 | 0.4 | |
| 33 | Neighbor Management | 16.0 | 1.4 | |
| 34 | Neighbor FSM | 6.0 | 0.4 | FSM code more concentrated |
| 35 | Hello processing | 3.0 | 0.3 | |
| 36 | Designated router election | 7.0 | 0.7 | |
| 37 | Packet Processing | 20.0 | 2.1 | |
| 38 | Packet validation | 4.0 | 0.4 | |
| 39 | Packet parsing | 8.0 | 0.8 | |
| 40 | Packet generation | 6.0 | 0.7 | |
| 41 | Authentication | 2.0 | 0.2 | |
| 42 | | | | |

**Figure 8.1: Example initial project plan**

To get a decently accurate project plan, the design should ideally include a breakdown detailed enough that all of the individual subtasks have estimates in the range of person-days or (low) person-weeks. A task with a higher estimate implies that the relevant function still has some question marks associated with it.

As an example, Figure 8.1 shows a (fictional) project plan for an implementation of a routing protocol. The plan has been put together in a straightforward spreadsheet, rather than a dedicated piece of planning software, because this best illustrates the core of what's going on.

There's a few things that are worth pointing out in this example.

- The major sections in the plan correspond to components in the overall architecture of the product, and the individual task lines correspond to particular subcomponents. From this it's clear that the project has already had some design thought put into it.
- The individual tasks have been estimated in terms of both resource

days (for an average developer) and lines of code. Most of the time there's a close equivalence between the two (around 10 days to implement 1000 lines of code), but some particular tasks are different.

- Various spreadsheet features have been used to make the plan as convenient as possible to read (analogously to naming conventions in code).
  - Indentation is used to indicate components and sub-components.
  - Grouping of components and sub-components allows summary information to be easily displayed, by collapsing the appropriate grouping levels.
  - Derived numbers such as sub-totals are highlighted (in blue italics here).

Of course, a detailed and thorough project plan isn't always achievable in the real world, and so the project plan has to cope with the uncertainty involved in less granular estimates. This is likely to involve a number of "plan B" scenarios (see section 8.4, "Replanning").

- Prototype key areas of uncertainty in the design to confirm that the suggested technical approach is likely to work and to scale appropriately.
- Defer functionality to a later release; as such, it's worth identifying early on which are core product features and which are "WIBNIs" ("Wouldn't It Be Nice If …").
- Defer some testing to a later phase—while planning for the expected consequences of this, such as higher support loads, more patches, reduced reputation etc.
- Move the release dates, again allowing for potential consequences (lost customers, penalty clauses, missed market opportunities).
- Add more resource to the project, provided that this is really going to help, rather than distract and dilute the core project team (which is all too common when manpower is added to a late project).

As described in the previous section, it's also important to bear in mind the statistical nature of estimates. Across the entire project, if the over-estimations and under-estimations balance out, then the project will be in pretty good shape. On the other hand, if there is a consistent bias in the estimates (and such a bias is bound to be in the direction of under-estimation), then that puts the project in jeopardy.

However, the more common reason for project disasters is forgetting an entire task. Sometimes this is a low-level technical task that gets missed because of a miscommunication between the designers; more often, it's a task that's not part of the core of the project but which is still vital to shipping the software out of the door.

Here's a list of peripheral tasks that can take a stunning amount of resource, and are often forgotten in the grand plan.

- Holidays, illness and staff turnover.
- Personnel matters: reviews, appraisals, staff meetings.
- Setting up and running the build system (see subsection 4.6.4, "Building the Code") and other systems (see subsection 4.6.2, "Other Tracking Systems").
- Ramping up on new technologies.
- Installing, managing and fixing test machines.
- Packaging and delivery (see subsection 4.6.5, "Delivering the Code").
- Documentation and training.
- Initial support, particularly for beta releases.
- Interactions with sales and marketing; for example, setting up and running a decent demo can lose weeks of project team resource.
- Internationalization and localization, including (for example) early UI freezes to allow time for translation (see section 4.2, "Internationalization").

In the end, the actual *coding* phase of a software project forms a minority of the time spent.

The key tool to deal with the risk of a forgotten task is *contingency*—keeping a pot of time in the project plan that can be used to mop up these unexpected obstacles (or to mop up the effects of a consistent under-estimation). The size of this pot can vary from 10% to 30% or even higher, depending on how predictable the project is.

If the project is a "cookie cutter" project, very similar in objective to a number of previous projects, then the contingency can be kept low. If the project involves a new team, new technologies, new hardware, new tools—all of these factors increase the amount of contingency needed. After the project, how the contingency pot was used provides lots of useful information for the next project that follows in this one's footsteps.

Returning to our previous example plan, we can now update it to include all of activities over and above writing the code (Figure 8.2). This includes the various test phases for the product (see section 6.1, "How"), together with a collection of the extra activities mentioned above.

This example plan includes quite a large pot for "management", so it's worth exploring what's included. This covers all of time needed for formal reviews or appraisals, plus time taken in teaching and mentoring the team.

| 1 2 3 | | A | B | C | D |
|---|---|---|---|---|---|
| | 1 | Task | Original Estimate | | Notes |
| | 2 | | Days | kLoC | |
| | 3 | **Total** | **583.5** | | |
| | 4 | Design/Code/Unit Test | 203.5 | 24.1 | |
| | 5 | Framework | 31.0 | 3.3 | |
| | 11 | Config/Management | 48.5 | 8.4 | |
| | 18 | Link State Processing | 55.0 | 5.5 | |
| | 27 | Route Calculation | 33.0 | 3.4 | |
| | 33 | Neighbor Management | 16.0 | 1.4 | |
| | 37 | Packet Processing | 20.0 | 2.1 | |
| | 42 | Test | 100.0 | | |
| | 43 | Functional Verification | 65.0 | | |
| | 44 | Mainline function | 15.0 | | |
| | 45 | Error processing | 10.0 | | |
| | 46 | Inter-area testing | 10.0 | | |
| | 47 | AS boundary tests | 15.0 | | |
| | 48 | MIB & management tests | 15.0 | | |
| | 49 | System Test | 35.0 | | |
| | 50 | Interoperability test | 15.0 | | |
| | 51 | Scalability tests | 10.0 | | |
| | 52 | Link failure tests | 10.0 | | |
| | 53 | Non-Development | 56.0 | | |
| | 54 | Build system | 15.0 | | |
| | 55 | Deliveries | 9.0 | | |
| | 56 | Documentation | 15.0 | | |
| | 57 | Ramp-up | 9.0 | | |
| | 58 | Sales support | 8.0 | | |
| | 59 | Overhead | 164.0 | | |
| | 60 | Management | 80.0 | | |
| | 61 | Illness | 10.0 | | |
| | 62 | Vacations | 50.0 | | |
| | 63 | Public holidays | 24.0 | | |
| | 64 | Contingency | 60.0 | | |
| | 65 | Unassigned | 60.0 | | |

**Figure 8.2: Fully burdened example plan**

It includes the time needed for assessing whether the project is running to plan or not, and to gather and analyse the metrics that lead up to that assessment. It also includes the time spent being the ambassador for the project to the rest of the organization—presenting status information, interacting with other teams, dealing with equipment logistics and so on.

With all of these tasks included under the management heading, a useful rule of thumb is that it takes roughly one day per person per week. This means that teams with more than five people tend to have weak points, unless some aspects of this management role are shared out with other members of the team. It is possible to squeeze by with less time spent on management, but in the long term the development of the team and the code will suffer.

# 8.2  Task Division

*fungible /adj./ replaceable by another identical item; mutually interchangeable[1].*

Programmers are not fungible. Firstly and most importantly, the range of skill levels for programmers range hugely—the best can be many times more productive than the average, and the worst can actually incur a net loss[2]. Even among software engineers of equivalent skill, some will have particular areas of specialty.

These factors induce yet another challenge when planning a project: how to divide up the various tasks of the project among the development team.

To deal with the overall variance of productivity among the various team members, it's important be clear about what units the plan is in:

- If task estimates are all quoted in terms of a standard "average developer-day", then the amount of calendar time needed to complete a task will depend on who's assigned to the task.
- If task estimates are quoted in terms of how long the specifically-assigned developer will take to complete the task, then calendar time is easier to calculate but changing task allocations is more complicated.

Either approach is feasible, but mixing up the two is a recipe for disaster.

In the short term, dealing with people's particular skills is much easier—just assign the team members to the tasks that they are good at. This hugely reduces the risks: to the experienced developer, repeating a type of task they've done before is a "cookie cutter" experience; to a novice team member, the same task is the cutting edge (see subsection 3.2.5, "Avoiding the Cutting Edge")

In the longer term, however, this is a short-sighted approach. If the same team member always does a particular type of task, then they may get bored and leave—at which point, the team is in trouble because there's no-one else who can do that task. As such, it's often a good idea to pair up an expert in a particular area with another team member who can learn from them.

Returning once again to our sample plan (Figure 8.3), the relevant

---

1    Concise Oxford English Dictionary, eleventh edition.

2    Their work can be so poor that it has to be abandoned and redone from scratch by someone more competent.

| | | A | B | C | D | |
|---|---|---|---|---|---|---|
| | 1 | Task | Person | Original | Estimate | |
| | 2 | | | Days | kLoC | |
| | 3 | **Total** | | ***583.5*** | | |
| | 4 | Design/Code/Unit Test | | *203.5* | *24.1* | |
| | 5 | Framework | | *31.0* | *3.3* | |
| | 11 | Config/Management | | *49.5* | *8.4* | |
| | 12 | SNMP parsing | ANO | 4.0 | 0.5 | |
| | 13 | MIB processing | | *7.0* | 3.0 | |
| | 15 | Data structure walking | JHC | 5.5 | 0.5 | |
| | 16 | Command line processing | | *12.0* | 2.0 | |
| | 17 | Design | JQB | 2.0 | | |
| | 18 | Design review | DMD | 0.5 | | |
| | 19 | Code | JQB | 5.0 | | |
| | 20 | Code review | DMD | 1.0 | | |
| | 21 | Unit test | JQB | 3.5 | | |
| | 22 | Display code | | *13.0* | 1.4 | |
| | 24 | Logging framework | | *7.0* | 1.0 | |
| | 26 | Link State Processing | | *55.0* | *5.5* | |
| | 27 | LSDB management | | *8.0* | 0.8 | |
| | 29 | Flooding | | *7.5* | 0.8 | |
| | 31 | LSA processing | | *17.0* | 1.7 | |
| | 32 | Design | ANO | 3.0 | | |
| | 33 | Design review | JHC | 1.0 | | |
| | 34 | Code | ANO | 6.0 | | |
| | 35 | Code review | JHC | 1.5 | | |
| | 36 | Unit test | ANO | 5.5 | | |
| | 37 | Local interface processing | DMD | 2.0 | 0.4 | |
| | 38 | Interface FSM | | *6.0* | 0.3 | |
| | 40 | Stub areas | | *7.0* | 0.7 | |
| | 42 | Not-so-stubby-areas | JHC | 4.0 | 0.4 | |
| | 43 | External route processing | JHC | 3.5 | 0.4 | |
| | 44 | Route Calculation | | *33.0* | *3.4* | |
| | 45 | SPF calculation | | *11.0* | 0.8 | |
| | 47 | Area boundary processing | | *7.5* | 1.0 | |
| | 49 | AS boundary processing | ANO | 5.5 | 0.7 | |
| | 50 | AS external route calculation | ANO | 5.0 | 0.5 | |
| | 51 | Route table publish | JHC | 4.0 | 0.4 | |
| | 52 | Neighbor Management | | *16.0* | *1.4* | |
| | 56 | Packet Processing | | *20.0* | *2.1* | |

**Figure 8.3: Example plan including task allocations**

updates are as follows.

- The larger and more significant development tasks have been broken down into more detail, splitting out separate tasks for low-level design, design review, code, code review and unit test. (Only a few of these breakdowns are shown in the diagram for space reasons.)
- An extra column indicates which member of the team has assigned to each task; in this case, the team involves three developers (JQB, ANO and JHC) and a manager (DMD).
- A summary table at the bottom of the spreadsheet indicates how

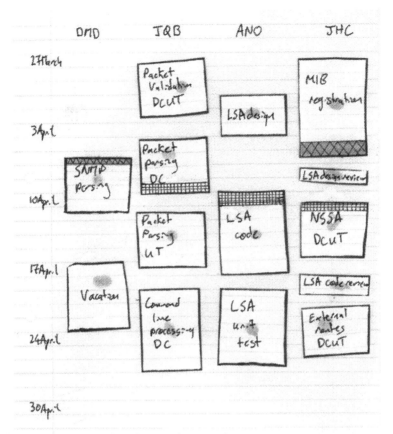

**Figure 8.4: Primitive Gantt chart technique**

much activity has been allocated to each member of the team (not shown in the diagram). This is useful as a quick guide to indicate who is potentially over-booked.

Once some specific tasks have been assigned to particular team members, all of the remaining tasks need to be assigned times and people—in other words, the project needs to have a rough timeline, in the form of a Gantt chart or equivalent. There are a number of software products that aim to help with this, but I've generally found that a simple paper-based approach works well. Starting with sheets of lined paper:

- Decide on a scale—say, one line per day, or two lines for a week.
- Write out a grid with dates down the left hand side of the paper (in accordance with the scale just decided on) and with the names of team members across the top of the paper.

- If there's a hard deadline, draw a big black line across the page at the relevant place.
- Using more lined paper and a pair of scissors, cut out a little rectangle of paper for each task in the plan. The rectangle should be roughly the same width as the columns drawn on the first piece of paper (the ones labelled with the names of team members), and should be the same height as the estimate you've got for the corresponding task. (If the rectangles are more than a few lines high, the scale is wrong or the tasks in the plan aren't fine-grained enough).
- Put a small piece of blu-tack on the back of each rectangle, and stick them onto the main piece of paper with no overlaps. The column each rectangle goes in indicates who's going to do the task; the rows it covers indicate when the task will be done.
- Make sure each person's column has a few gaps in it, to allow wiggle room for illness, slippage, and other unforeseen events. Leave bigger gaps for less capable team members, who are more likely to overrun on any particular task.

This approach makes any of the common scheduling problems immediately visible:

- If you've got any rectangles left over, you've not assigned all the tasks.
- If any of the rectangles overlap, then some poor team member is over-assigned.
- If there are large swathes of the underlying piece of paper visible, then some team member is under-assigned.
- If any of the rectangle are below the big black line, then your plan doesn't hit your deadline.

Simple but effective.

# 8.3  Dependencies

In any project plan, there are some tasks that need to be completed before others can be started. This is glaringly obvious in civil engineering projects (see chapter 3, "Design")—there's no way to build the roof of a building before the walls are done, and the walls can't get done until the foundation is built.

Similar considerations apply for software engineering projects, but they are typically less important, and there are a couple of key techniques that help to bypass the ordering requirement that dependencies impose.

The main technique is to rely on the separation of interfaces and imple-

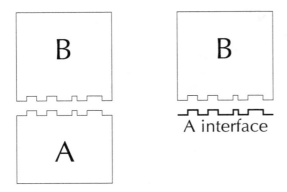

**Figure 8.5: Building to an interface**

mentations (see section 3.1, "Interfaces and Implementations"): if the interface of component A is provided well in advance of the implementation of A, then a component B which relies on A can still be built in parallel with A, using that interface.

If this is done, it's important to make sure that the implementers of both components stay in communication during the development process. During the implementation of component A, there's a chance that the details of its interface might need to change somewhat, and those changes need to be reflected in component B. Conversely, the implementer of component B might find that their job would be much easier if the interface of A were changed just a little bit, and discussion with the implementer of A will reveal whether this is feasible or not.

This technique of interface/implementation separation can also be extended if the system as a whole involves a comprehensive internal test framework (see section 6.5, "Design for Testability"). With just the interface of component A to hand, the implementer of component B can get as far as compiling their code, but no further. However, if an independent test harness for component B is built, that framework can effectively provide an alternative implementation for the interface to A, allowing testing of B before A is written. The test implementation of A can and should be shared with the developer who is implementing the real component A, to avoid nasty surprises when the code gets integrated together.

For the dependencies that do exist in a software project, there's a simple extension to the paper approach to Gantt charts described in the previous section (see section 8.2, "Task Division"). If task A has to be completed before task B can start, then highlight the bottom edge of the task rectangle for A with a colour, and highlight the top edge of B with the same

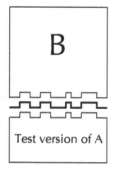

**Figure 8.6: Test driver**

colour. Any broken dependencies then show up as a top edge appearing above a bottom edge in the same colour.

## 8.4  Replanning

With the best will in the world, there comes a point in the lifecycle of many (most?) software development projects where it becomes clear that things are not on track—few plans survive contact with reality completely unscathed.

This first step in dealing with this situation to figure out the extent of the problem, and confirm that there isn't enough contingency to cope. Getting a different pair of eyes to look things over can help a lot with this—explaining the situation to someone else can also expose the self-deceptions you've hidden from yourself.

Once it's clear that these is a problem, it's vital to face up to the problem as soon as possible, and to be realistic about what can actually be achieved by when. As with bugs in the software, it's much easier to deal with problems in the plan the sooner they are raised and dealt with. Despite this, it's surprisingly common that a missed deadline is only admitted to a week before it happens, even when the impending doom of the project has been obvious to all concerned for months. Raising the problem sooner rather than later allows everyone involved to put contingency plans in place.

So what possibilities are there for these contingency plans?
- Change the delivery dates, if this is possible.
- Change the deliverables, to defer less important functionality to a later release.
- Reduce the quality (typically by reducing/deferring testing), although this counts as a deliverable of sorts (see section 2.3,

"Implicit Requirements").

- Add resource to the project. Adding personnel to the core team at a late date is likely to have a negative effect, because of the time taken ramping up and communicating with the new team members. However, it may be possible to reduce any extra commitments of the core team or to find easily separable subtasks which can be hived off to someone external without that external person needing to ramp up on the whole project.

For all of these possibilities, the replanning exercise has also got to take into account any knock-on effects on subsequent projects or other teams.

# 9  RUNNING A PROJECT

There's more to project management than just coming up with a comprehensive project plan. This chapter discusses the ongoing process of running a project, with the aim of turning that plan into reality.

## 9.1  Tracking

Once the planning for a software project is done, the business of actually implementing the software can kick off in earnest. The job of the project manager is not over, though—the progress of the project in reality has to be tracked against the predictions of the plan. This tracking allows progress to be measured, and makes it possible to determine whether the project is in trouble (see section 8.4, "Replanning").

The responsibility for tracking the status of the project doesn't just rest with the project manager, though. Each of the members of the team has to be able to report their own status, and to analyse what they're spending their time on. Often, supposedly "absorbable" tasks like running the builds, preparing releases, or answering pre-sales enquiries can take up a lot of time, and it's important that the project manager knows about these ancillary activities (if only so they can allow more time for it in the *next* project, see subsection 8.1.2, "Project Estimation").

### 9.1.1  Metrics

In order to be able to extrapolate the status of the project into the future, we need quantitative measurements—*metrics*.

The most important metric during software development is to determine how much of each subtask has been done. This might be the number of lines of code written, as compared to the expected number of lines of

| Task | Person | Estimate Days | Current Status Done | Current Status ToDo | Gain | week: 2006-04-17 | 2006-04-10 | 2006-04-03 |
|---|---|---|---|---|---|---|---|---|
| **Total** | | **583.5** | **181.0** | **409.5** | **-7.00** | **20.00** | **20.00** | **20.00** |
| Design/Code/Unit Test | | 203.5 | 117.00 | 89.50 | -3.00 | | | |
| Framework | | 31.0 | 28.00 | 0.00 | 3.00 | | | |
| Config/Management | | 48.5 | 47.00 | 4.00 | -2.50 | | | |
| Link State Processing | | 55.0 | 41.00 | 17.50 | -3.50 | | | |
| LSDB management | | 8.0 | 7.50 | 0.00 | 0.50 | | | |
| Flooding | | 7.5 | 10.50 | 0.00 | -3.00 | | | |
| LSA processing | | 17.0 | 15.25 | 3.00 | -1.25 | | | |
| Design | AND | 3.0 | 2.75 | 0.00 | 0.25 | | | 0.75 |
| Design review | JHC | 1.0 | 0.75 | 0.00 | 0.25 | | | 0.75 |
| Code | AND | 6.0 | 6.50 | 0.00 | -0.50 | 0.50 | 5.00 | 1.00 |
| Code review | JHC | 1.5 | 1.75 | 0.00 | -0.25 | 1.75 | | |
| Unit test | AND | 5.5 | 3.50 | 3.00 | -1.00 | 3.50 | | |
| Local interface processing | DMD | 2.0 | 1.75 | 0.00 | 0.25 | | | |
| Interface FSM | | 6.0 | 6.00 | 0.00 | 0.00 | | | |
| Stub areas | | 7.0 | 0.00 | 7.00 | 0.00 | | | |
| Not-so-stubby-areas | | 4.0 | 0.00 | 4.00 | 0.00 | | | |
| External route processing | JHC | 3.5 | 0.00 | 3.50 | 0.00 | | | |
| Route Calculation | | 33.0 | 1.00 | 32.00 | 0.00 | | | |
| Neighbor Management | | 16.0 | 0.00 | 16.00 | 0.00 | | | |
| Packet Processing | | 20.0 | 0.00 | 20.00 | 0.00 | | | |
| Test | | 100.0 | 0.00 | 100.00 | 0.00 | | | |
| Non-Development | | 56.0 | 16.00 | 44.00 | -4.00 | | | |
| Overhead | | 164.0 | 44.00 | 120.00 | 0.00 | | | |
| Management | | 80.0 | 19.00 | 61.00 | 0.00 | 1.00 | 1.25 | 0.50 |
| Illness | | 10.0 | 2.00 | 8.00 | 0.00 | | | |
| Vacations | | 50.0 | 15.00 | 35.00 | 0.00 | | | 5.00 |
| Public holidays | | 24.0 | 8.00 | 16.00 | 0.00 | | | |
| Contingency | | 60.0 | 4.00 | 56.00 | 0.00 | | | |
| Unassigned | | 60.0 | 0.00 | 54.00 | 6.00 | | | |
| Test plan | | 0.0 | 4.00 | 2.00 | -6.00 | 2.00 | 2.00 | |

**Figure 9.1: Example spreadsheet with ongoing task tracking information**

code for the finished component. More likely, this will involve the number of man-days spent so far and the expected number of man-days left to do on the task. Either way, until there is working code, there are few other things that can be measured.

Once again, we can illustrate this with our example project spreadsheet (Figure 9.1). The key things to observe with this iteration are as follows.

- Time tracking for the team on a week-by-week basis has been added on the right hand side of the spreadsheet, and is summarized in the "Done" column. (A more sophisticated spreadsheet might track team members individually).
- The "To Do" column is regularly revisited so that it holds a current best estimate of how much effort still remains for any particular task.
- The "Gain" column holds a running track of how the progress of the project is going in comparison with the original estimates. Comparing this number with the amount of contingency remaining gives a good indication of whether the overall project schedule is at risk.
- Various subtotals are included to make it obvious when incorrect data has been added (which is easy to do). For example, the amount of time spent each week should always add up to 20, as there are four team members working five days a week.

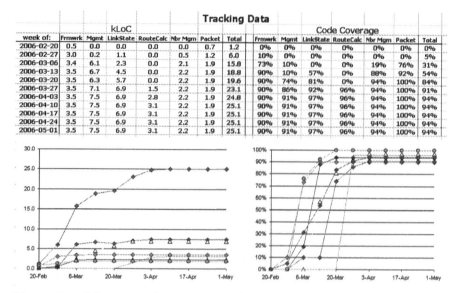

**Tracking Data**

| week of: | kLoC | | | | | | | Code Coverage | | | | | | |
|---|---|---|---|---|---|---|---|---|---|---|---|---|---|---|
| | Frmwrk | Mgmt | LinkState | RouteCalc | Nbr Mgm | Packet | Total | Frmwrk | Mgmt | LinkState | RouteCalc | Nbr Mgm | Packet | Total |
| 2006-02-20 | 0.5 | 0.0 | 0.0 | 0.0 | 0.0 | 0.7 | 1.2 | 0% | 0% | 0% | 0% | 0% | 0% | 0% |
| 2006-02-27 | 3.0 | 0.2 | 1.1 | 0.0 | 0.5 | 1.2 | 6.0 | 10% | 0% | 0% | 0% | 0% | 0% | 5% |
| 2006-03-06 | 3.4 | 6.1 | 2.3 | 0.0 | 2.1 | 1.9 | 15.8 | 73% | 10% | 0% | 0% | 19% | 76% | 31% |
| 2006-03-13 | 3.5 | 6.7 | 4.5 | 0.0 | 2.2 | 1.9 | 18.8 | 90% | 10% | 57% | 0% | 88% | 92% | 54% |
| 2006-03-20 | 3.5 | 6.3 | 5.7 | 0.0 | 2.2 | 1.9 | 19.6 | 90% | 74% | 81% | 0% | 94% | 100% | 84% |
| 2006-03-27 | 3.5 | 7.1 | 6.9 | 1.5 | 2.2 | 1.9 | 23.1 | 90% | 86% | 92% | 96% | 94% | 100% | 91% |
| 2006-04-03 | 3.5 | 7.5 | 6.9 | 2.8 | 2.2 | 1.9 | 24.8 | 90% | 91% | 97% | 96% | 94% | 100% | 94% |
| 2006-04-10 | 3.5 | 7.5 | 6.9 | 3.1 | 2.2 | 1.9 | 25.1 | 90% | 91% | 97% | 96% | 94% | 100% | 94% |
| 2006-04-17 | 3.5 | 7.5 | 6.9 | 3.1 | 2.2 | 1.9 | 25.1 | 90% | 91% | 97% | 96% | 94% | 100% | 94% |
| 2006-04-24 | 3.5 | 7.5 | 6.9 | 3.1 | 2.2 | 1.9 | 25.1 | 90% | 91% | 97% | 96% | 94% | 100% | 94% |
| 2006-05-01 | 3.5 | 7.5 | 6.9 | 3.1 | 2.2 | 1.9 | 25.1 | 90% | 91% | 97% | 96% | 94% | 100% | 94% |

**Figure 9.2: Metric tracking in example spreadsheet**

- A missing task ("Test plan") has been identified, and added as an additional subtask under the "Contingency" section (reducing the unassigned contingency appropriately).

With working code in hand, there are a number of other metrics which can help to assess the status of a project.

- Number of lines of code (or more specifically, number of non-blank, non-comment lines of code).
- Number of functions.
- Number of branch-points in the code (depending on coding standards, this can often be accurately approximated by counting the number of { characters in a code file, for C-like languages at least).
- Bugs found at review, and their classification.
- Bugs found during testing, and their classification.
- Speed and size of the code for key scenarios.
- Number of test cases successfully executed.
- Amount of coverage of the code during testing.
- Amount of time taken to fix bugs (average, maximum).

For any metric, it is important to understand that people will change their behaviour to optimize whatever metric is being concentrated on.

With this in mind, the list of potential metrics given above has a corresponding list of counter-productive behaviours that could be induced by concentrating too hard on each metric.

- Number of man-days left: components will be coded as fast as possible, without regard for how good the code is.
- Number of lines or branch-points in the code: code will be copied and pasted rather than encapsulated.
- Number of functions: the code will have many layers of shell functions that do no processing.
- Bugs found at review or during testing: code development will slow to a glacial pace, as the developers exhibit excessive caution.
- Speed and size of the code for key scenarios: the code will be incomprehensible because the very last drops of performance have been squeezed out of it, and the performance in other scenarios will drop (this is very common for graphics cards that get tuned for particular high-visibility benchmarks).
- Number of test cases successfully executed, or amount of coverage of the code during testing: the amount of time spent on the more important mainline tests will be lower than it should be (for example, testing odd timing windows often reveals important bugs but doesn't hit any new areas of the code).
- Amount of time taken to fix bugs: the fastest, least architectural, sticking-plaster fixes will be applied (see below).

In larger companies, organizationally mandated metrics can become applied in a completely inflexible manner, so that any benefit in optimizing for that metric is outweighed by its negative long-term effects.

An example is in order: in one large organization I encountered, the time taken to close out a bug report was closely monitored, and any bug open longer than two weeks was escalated way up the management hierarchy. The noble intent of this policy was to encourage responsiveness and good service for the customers. In practice the policy meant that the most short-sighted, fastest-to-implement fixes were always the ones that made it into the codebase. After a few years of this, the codebase was littering with special cases (see subsection 3.2.2, "Minimizing Special Cases") and copied and pasted code. If a bug report that involved corruption of a database record came in, the developers would restore the record from a backup, and close out the bug report—since investigating the underlying cause as to why a dozen records were getting corrupted each week would have taken far longer than the two week period that triggered the metric.

The same organization also had astonishingly high support costs, because the internal budgeting for the development of new code was completely separate from the budget for support: developers were positively encouraged to write poor code and ship it as fast as possible, because the support costs didn't show up in the cost calculations for the new features.

This last example illustrates the most influential metric of all: *money*—or its near-equivalent, time. In the end, software projects have to make money to pay the salaries of the developers.

On a smaller scale project, it's much easier to watch out for these kind of perverse behaviours creeping in. To avoid the problem in the first place, it's often useful to monitor different metrics that push people's behaviour in opposite directions and thus cancel out any psychological effect.

## 9.1.2 Feedback

The previous section described a number of potential metrics that can be used for tracking the health of a software development project.

The obvious and most important use of these numbers is to determine if the project is running smoothly, in order to extrapolate whether the deadlines and targets are all going to be reached.

However, the lower-level details of the figures can also provide a valuable source of feedback about the performance of the team. This can be monitored as the project progresses (for longer projects), or can be looked at separately in a project post-mortem.

After the fact, every project should be mined for information, to help to move future projects away from the trail-blazing scenario, closer to the "cookie cutter" scenario. Look over the numbers to see how the estimation errors were distributed, and what the contingency pot ended up being used for—so the next project can have explicit, planned tasks for the tasks that were missed, together with a better confidence level on the estimates for them.

To make this information as useful as possible, it helps to distinguish between the changes in the plan that occurred because the original estimates were wrong or missing some tasks, and the changes that happened because of externally imposed changes (such as a change in the specification, or a member of the team leaving unexpectedly). Knowing the difference between when the goalposts have been missed, and when the goalposts have been moved, makes the next plan more accurate—so it's important to preserve the numbers in the original plan and refer back to them later.

The performance of individual developers can also be revealed by the underlying numbers—bug counts per line of code, time taken to write each line of code. These concrete numbers can help the project manager to motivate the team members in the directions they need to develop. For

| | Task | Estimate | | Current Status | | | Actual | Notes |
|---|---|---|---|---|---|---|---|---|
| | | Days | kLoC | Done | ToDo | Gain | kLoc | |
| 3 | **Total** | **583.5** | | **596.5** | **0.0** | **-13.0** | | |
| 4 | Design/Code/Unit Test | 203.5 | 24.1 | 213.0 | 0.0 | -9.5 | 25.1 | |
| 5 | Framework | 31.0 | 3.3 | 28.0 | 0.0 | 3.0 | 3.5 | |
| 11 | Config/Management | 48.5 | 8.4 | 55.0 | 0.0 | -6.5 | 7.5 | |
| 26 | Link State Processing | 55.0 | 5.5 | 62.0 | 0.0 | -7.0 | 6.9 | |
| 44 | Route Calculation | 33.0 | 3.4 | 33.0 | 0.0 | 0.0 | 3.1 | |
| 52 | Neighbor Management | 16.0 | 1.4 | 20.0 | 0.0 | -4.0 | 2.2 | |
| 56 | Packet Processing | 20.0 | 2.1 | 15.0 | 0.0 | 5.0 | 1.9 | Recycled test code from RIP |
| 61 | Test | 100.0 | | 108.0 | 0.0 | -2.0 | | |
| 62 | Functional Verification | 65.0 | | 61.0 | 0.0 | 4.0 | | |
| 68 | System Test | 35.0 | | 47.0 | 0.0 | -12.0 | | Box setup for interop tests |
| 72 | Non-Development | 56.0 | | 64.0 | 0.0 | -8.0 | | |
| 73 | Build system | 15.0 | | 22.0 | 0.0 | -7.0 | | |
| 74 | Deliveries | 9.0 | | 8.0 | 0.0 | 1.0 | | |
| 75 | Documentation | 15.0 | | 21.0 | 0.0 | -6.0 | | Config & Mgmt guide slipped |
| 76 | Ramp-up | 9.0 | | 7.0 | 0.0 | 2.0 | | |
| 77 | Sales support | 8.0 | | 6.0 | 0.0 | 2.0 | | |
| 78 | Overhead | 164.0 | | 167.0 | 0.0 | -3.0 | | |
| 79 | Management | 80.0 | | 86.0 | 0.0 | -6.0 | | |
| 80 | Illness | 10.0 | | 7.0 | 0.0 | 3.0 | | |
| 81 | Vacations | 50.0 | | 50.0 | 0.0 | 0.0 | | |
| 82 | Public holidays | 24.0 | | 24.0 | 0.0 | 0.0 | | |
| 83 | Contingency | 60.0 | | 44.5 | 0.0 | 15.5 | | |
| 84 | Unassigned | 60.0 | | 0.0 | 0.0 | 60.0 | | |
| 85 | Test plan | 0.0 | | 8.0 | 0.0 | -8.0 | | |
| 86 | Opaque LSA support | 0.0 | | 20.0 | 0.0 | -20.0 | | Requirement added 2006-04-07 |
| 87 | MIB agent test tool | 0.0 | | 5.5 | 0.0 | -5.5 | | |
| 88 | katz-yeung MIB | 0.0 | | 11.0 | 0.0 | -11.0 | | Requirement added 2006-05-02 |

**Figure 9.3: Post-mortem of example plan (changes in specification indicated by gray background)**

example, junior developers often fall into the trap of writing code blazingly quickly, but which has a much higher bug count than more experienced developers. In this situation, being able to show the developer their bug rate as compared to the average (together with the fix time associated with that bug rate) can help to convince them to slow down and take more care, in a way that doesn't involve recrimination and subjective opinion.

Similarly, the overall statistics for the project can give some indication of the performance of the project managers. Occasionally projects get awarded to the manager who comes up with the most aggressive, overly optimistic estimates[1]; a long-term calibration of the eventual outcome ensures that these managers can learn the error of their ways.

# 9.2 Time Management

With the complexities of project management comes an attendant problem for the project manager: time management. It's particularly common for new project managers to find themselves panicking as more and more tasks and issues pile up in their inbox.

At the core of the problem is a perennial trade-off between *important*

---

1 A friend of mine refers to these types as the "can-do cowboys".

tasks and *urgent* tasks. It's easy to get into a "fire-fighting" situation where the only things that get any attention are the ones that are due immediately; other vital tasks get ignored in the frenzy—at least until they too have a looming deadline.

The first step in dealing with the problem is to have a reliable system for tracking tasks and issues. This doesn't have to be high-tech—a paper list works fine—but there has to be no chance of anything ever getting lost from the system. Tasks and issues stay on the list until they're done, explicitly confirmed as no longer needed, or passed to someone else to deal with. New things go onto the system immediately, so there's less chance of an issue being forgotten on the walk back from a conference room to a desk[2].

The next step is to make sure that the tracking system doesn't get completely crufted up with important but not yet vital tasks. Revisiting the list on a regular basis—say once a week—to check on the status of the less urgent items helps to keep them fresh in the memory. However, in the end the only way to reduce the size of the task list is to actually do some of the tasks—so reserve some time for a background task or two each week.

One analogy can help to clarify both the problem and the heuristics for solving it, at least for project managers with a software background: scheduling algorithms. Modern pre-emptive operating systems face a very similar challenge in determining how processor time-slices should be assigned to different tasks. As with project management, there are high priority tasks, low priority tasks, interrupts, time deadlines, and a measurable cost for context switching. With that in mind, it's worth reading about some of the techniques that operating systems use to ensure that everything gets done eventually—UNIX systems and Linux in particular are good subjects for study because of their tradition of documented algorithms and availability of source code (and this is useful knowledge for a software professional anyway, see subsection 9.4.1, "Technical Fundamentals").

# 9.3 Running a Team

For any software project above a certain size, running the project also involves running the team that is implementing the project. This can be difficult—the software industry certainly has its share of prima-donna programmers, loose cannons and work-shy drones—but the calibre of the development team is a vital factor affecting the quality of the final code.

---

2   Paper lists have the advantage in this kind of situation, being more easily portable.

## 9.3.1 Explaining Decisions

An important thing to understand about managing a team of software engineers is that things go much more smoothly when you explain the reasons for your decisions.

It might be possible to tell team members just to do what they're told in other industries, but software engineers are intelligent enough that this doesn't go down well. Developers like to believe that they are completely rational people; explaining the motivations for your decisions allows you to leverage this (belief in their own) rationality.

The developers on your team might not always agree with you, but if you explore all of the reasons for choosing between two different approaches, the difference in opinion normally boils down a choice between whether factor X or factor Y is more important. With that understood, it's much easier to either fashion a compromise or to convince the developer to follow your approach without grumbling. This openness is what prevents management from degenerating into an "us" versus "them" situation.

## 9.3.2 Make Everything Into Code

Good programmers enjoy writing code. This observation is the key to a useful secret for getting programmers to be enthusiastic about some of the less interesting parts of software development (or at least to be willing to do them)—make those parts look like writing code.

The parts of software development that developers find less interesting are the ones that involve tedious manual processes—collating data, tracking metrics and so on. But tedious manual processes are exactly the things that can be automated by a judicious application of a little bit of code—just what programmers enjoy.

Allowing time for the team to put together these kind of small process tools (Perl scripts, Excel macros etc.) improves the morale of the team and in the long run ensures more accurate and reliable implementations of the various processes involved.

Some examples:
- Testing: A regressible test framework for automated testing involves writing a bunch more code; a set of tests that are run by hand doesn't. Guess which one programmers enjoy more.
- Planning: Estimating tasks and tracking progress (see subsection 9.1.1, "Metrics") often involves a lot of mechanical processes for checking code size and coverage and so on, which can be scripted.

- Build System: Taking the time to automate the build system so that it copes with all eventualities, and even automatically tracks down the culprits who break the build (by correlating what code has broken with who last changed it) can save lots of the build-master's time and sanity.

With this approach, it's worth emphasizing that the normal ideals of what makes good code apply to these ancillary areas too. A good developer wouldn't copy and paste large sections of the product code, so there's no excuse for them to do it in test code or build scripts either. Similarly, everything should be version controlled, backed up, commented—and maybe even reviewed by other members of the team.

## 9.3.3 Tuning Development Processes

Poor logistics have the potential to seriously annoy a software development team. Programmers pride themselves on being intelligent; this is combined with training that emphasizes hunting down and eliminating unnecessary and inefficient code. This mindset stays in play when they have to deal with all of the processes and systems that go along with software development in an organization—bug reporting systems, status tracking systems, official documentation formats, mandatory ticketing systems etc.

As a project manager, it's easy to forget the realities of life at the coal face and it's sometimes difficult to predict the day-to-day consequences of new processes and systems (see subsection 4.6.2, "Other Tracking Systems"). The team members are usually pretty quick to point out any shortcomings; as a project manager, it's your job to listen to your team and to tune the processes as much as possible.

Once developers get into the habit of the development processes, they often find that the processes are not as much of a burden as they originally thought. If there are still concerns, examine the overhead involved in the processes—examine all of the steps involved in fixing a single one-line typo in a source code file.

- How many distinct steps are there?
- How many of those steps involve copying and pasting information?
- How many of the steps involve a delay, and for how long?
- How many of the steps involve another person (and so may be delayed until they read their email)?

If the total overhead is excessive, it becomes a big barrier to the developers' motivation to fix things.

Where it's not possible to completely automate a process, it is worth explaining to the team what the value of the process is (continuing the earlier theme; see subsection 9.3.1, "Explaining Decisions"). If they understand the rationale, they are more motivated to comply with the process and are more able to suggest modifications to an arduous process that preserve its value while reducing its annoyance level.

# 9.4  Personnel Development

The most significant factor in software quality is the quality of the person writing the software. Hiring the best developers, keeping the best developers happy once they're on board, and training new programmers up to become the best developers are the ways to achieve a high calibre development staff.

Developing the development staff is an ongoing activity that proceeds at a number of levels. Obviously, during the course of a project the members of the development team will naturally acquire knowledge about the particular problem domain of the project, and the tools and techniques used in building the system. This domain-specific knowledge needs to be spread around the team (see subsection 5.1.3, "Education", see section 6.2, "Who and When") so that no single developer becomes a bottleneck or overly essential to the project. This is an aspect of team professionalism: the team should be able to continue even if one of its members were to be hit by a bus tomorrow.

Spreading around the knowledge of different aspects of the system also helps to inculcate a wider perspective in the developers—rather than just concentrating on their own little components, they are more likely to understand the system as a whole and how their component affects the overall final system.

## 9.4.1 Technical Fundamentals

It's important that new programmers acquire knowledge and experience of technical areas outside of the things that are immediately needed for the current project. There are several reasons for this:

- Future projects may need different skill sets, and may not have enough time for the development team to ramp up fully.
- The more experience a developer has of different technical areas (programming languages, operating systems, development tools, code control systems, bug tracking systems, ...) the more they are

able to spot the common patterns between these different areas, and to induct the key factors involved.

- The deeper knowledge a developer has of how underlying code and systems are implemented (APIs, libraries, operating systems), the better they get at debugging and understanding the foibles of those systems.
- If a developer is bored and not expanding their skill set and experience, they may begin to worry about being painted into a corner career-wise, and start looking for other jobs that have more prospects.

It's surprising how few new programmers have a thorough understanding of the underlying systems that their code relies on, even among those arriving with computer science degrees. As such, there are a number of core software ideas and technologies that new programmers should get a working knowledge of during their first couple of years.

My personal list is given below; different development sectors will obviously have different lists. However, it's always motivational to be able to explain why and when these pieces of knowledge can come in handy (given in parentheses below).

- How a compiler works. (Useful for determining what the problem is when it stops working, and to optimize the code for the best output from the compiler.)
- How the linker and loader work. (Again, useful to know when it stops working and to optimize things.)
- How central features of higher level languages are implemented—for example, how virtual functions and exceptions work in C++. (This is useful for debugging problems at the very lowest level; imagine debugging a crash in stripped binary with a bare-bones debugger.)
- How a operating system's scheduling algorithm works[3]. (Vital for ensuring the best performance of a software system as a whole.)
- Assembly language. (Being able to read assembler allows you to debug problems when the compiler or debugger has gone awry, and tune the very last drops of performance out pieces of code on the golden path.)
- Virtual memory, memory models and allocation algorithms—in other words, how `malloc` works. (Occasionally helpful to tune allocation patterns for performance, but much more commonly useful when debugging memory errors: a double `free` will often cause problems on a later call to `malloc`.)

---

3  This can even be useful elsewhere (see section 9.2, "Time Management").

- A scripting language such as the Bourne shell, or awk or Perl or Python or Ruby or .... (Having a scripting language at your disposal allows the easy automation of any number of ancillary tasks that show up around a codebase—building it, testing it, analysing it.)
- Regular expressions. (Regular expressions form a core part of most scripting languages, and allow swift manipulation of textual data for all sorts of ancillary tasks.)
- Multithreading, with its pros and cons (see section 4.3, "Multithreading") and key issues like deadly embraces and lock-ing hierarchies. (Knowing the issues makes it easier to debug the almost-intractable bugs that can show up with poorly designed multithreaded code. Easier, but not easy, sadly.)
- Networking protocols, IP and TCP especially. (For anything involv-ing networking, the least common denominator in debugging is to fire up the sniffer and look at the packets on the wire. Knowing what you're looking for helps enormously.)
- Internationalization and localization. (Any software that interacts with users should deal with these issues; otherwise, you're closing off a huge potential market—and one that's growing all the time. Also, thinking about internationalization can help clarify underly-ing design concepts (see section 4.2, "Internationalization").)
- Event-based GUI programming. (This is the core of how all of the everyday software for users works. In the unlikely event that you never have to write any user-facing software, that won't stop your friends and family asking you to help with theirs.)

## 9.4.2 Pragmatism

Once a software engineer has been trained up to be the very finest software engineer, with the highest standards of software quality and professionalism, comes the next step: training them not to be. Or to be more accurate: training them to understand when and how to drop their standards and let less-than-perfect code out of the door.

Software development is usually about selling software for money, directly or indirectly. Even on open-source projects, there is still an equiva-lent balance of resources that has to be considered, although it involves people's time and interest rather than money.

The economic aspect highlights the key judgement call: is the program-mer time spent developing a feature or fixing a bug going to be more than reflected in the amount of money that will eventually roll in the door?

Even for software with six-nines reliability, it can sometimes be worth letting sleeping bugs lie.

The type of software involved makes a huge qualitative difference to this judgement call. For a Flash animation game on a website, having an obscure bug that occasionally crashes the program isn't a big deal—after all, most users will probably just blame it on the failings of Internet Explorer. However, for software that controls a kidney dialysis machine, or a nuclear power plant, the cost/reward ratios are obviously a lot more significant.

This is obviously very hard to quantify. The developer time spent now may be easy to measure, but it's much harder to predict the number of developer hours induced in the future by taking a shortcut—and harder still to quantify[4] the reputation damage and consequent longer-term monetary damage associated with delivering less-than-perfect software.

However, just because the problem is quantitatively insoluble doesn't mean that these kind of factors shouldn't be tracked. As programmers become software engineers and then senior software engineers and team leaders, it becomes more and more important that they are able to assess the factors both for and against perfection.

An important point, though: it has to be an explicit, conscious choice to take a particular pragmatic approach—this is not the same as taking hacky shortcuts because the engineers aren't capable of doing it any other way.

---

4  Some areas of the six-nines world incur fines for loss of service—making it easier to quantify the costs of poor quality.

# INDEX

# COLOPHON

The photograph on the cover of this book was taken by the author at the Bayon temple in Angkor, Cambodia, in August 2005. Post-processing was performed with Adobe Photoshop Elements 3.

The cover as a whole was produced in Adobe Illustrator CS2.

The body text of the book is set in Adobe Caslon Pro, and the headings are set in Optima (except chapter titles, which are set in Times New Roman).

This book was originally written in the Texinfo format, and made available on the web at www.lurklurk.org.

The Texinfo source was semi-automatically converted to a tagged text format using a bespoke Perl script written by the author. The book as a whole was typeset in Adobe InDesign CS2, importing the tagged text.

The book's figures were originally produced using the Xfig drawing program. These were then converted to Adobe Illustrator CS2 and re-set.

The example project spreadsheet was created in NeoOffice and then exported to Microsoft Excel, where the screenshots were captured using Gadwin PrintScreen. The sample Gantt chart was scanned using a CanoScan 9950F scanner.

All of the processing for this book was performed on an Apple Powerbook G4.